To Susan—
Have fun +
Happy Knitting!

KNIT
IN NEW DIRECTIONS→

with

MYRA
WOOD

KNITINK

PUBLISHER • Alexis Yiorgos Xenakis

EDITOR • Elaine Rowley

MANAGING EDITOR • Karen Bright

TECHNICAL EDITOR • Rick Mondragon

KNITTING INSTRUCTION • Traci Bunkers • Sarah Peasley • Ginger Smith

ART DIRECTOR • Natalie Sorenson

PHOTOGRAPHER • Alexis Yiorgos Xenakis

STYLIST • Rick Mondragon

ASSISTANT STYLIST • Lisa Mannes

CHIEF EXECUTIVE OFFICER • Benjamin Levisay

DIRECTOR, PUBLISHING SERVICES • David Xenakis

TECHNICAL ILLUSTRATOR • Carol Skallerud

PRODUCTION DIRECTOR & COLOR SPECIALIST • Dennis Pearson

BOOK PRODUCTION MANAGER • Greg Hoogeveen

MARKETING MANAGER • Lisa Mannes

BOOKS DISTRIBUTION • Molly Bonestroo

MIS • Jason Bittner

FIRST PUBLISHED IN THE USA
IN 2014 BY XRX, INC.

COPYRIGHT © 2014 XRX, INC.

Pellon® is a registered trademark
of PCP Group, LLC

All rights reserved.
ISBN 13: 9781933064284

Produced in
Sioux Falls, South Dakota by

XRX, Inc.
PO Box 965
Sioux Falls, SD
57101-0965 USA

605.338.2450

Visit us online —
knittinguniverse.com

Printed in Hong Kong

KNIT

IN NEW DIRECTIONS

with

MYRA WOOD

photography by

ALEXIS XENAKIS

Welcome!

I have tons of fun and quite a journey in store for you!

Some of us like a lot of structure, others prefer as little as possible, but most people are somewhere in the middle. The exciting news is that you can approach creative knitting any way you like, from fully structured and preplanned to completely winging it. One is certain to suit your style.

We start off by investigating what creativity means and how it relates to knitting. Next we explore templates, including how to make them and how to use the ones in this book. Then I introduce techniques for strip, modular, creative short-row, Crazy-Quilt, and Freeform knitting — all accompanied by designs and instructions for one-of-a-kind garments and accessories. I include tips and tricks on fit and finish, including steaming, a Modified Mattress Stitch for seaming, finishing edges, and embellishment options.

The patterns are graded for specific sizes, with instructions on how to measure each piece and knit it accordingly. The book is full of suggestions and options for using the templates and techniques, allowing you to be as creative as you'd like.

Of course, you can also be a trailblazer and use the templates and other resources for any project you like. Feel free to explore possibilities on your own.

So get comfortable, and get ready for template-based creative knitting!

And most importantly — have fun!!

Creativity is about making mistakes...

...on purpose.

4

My patterns leave room for interpretation. I hope they empower you to try new things. Think of them more as basic recipes than as precise instructions.

I encourage you to make choices: yarn, template size, garment shape, and stitch patterns. It may take a bit of time for you to be comfortable with this approach, but stick with it and soon you'll begin to look at your knitting in a whole new way.

My hope is that this book becomes a template for your own creativity!

The road ahead

knit in new directions

Creative short rows

Crazy Quilt knitting

Freeform

a journey into creativity

So many times I see people handcuffed and hogtied by their own thoughts about what is "right." As if there's one right way to do something and they have to find it.

With creativity, there is no right. Creativity is about making mistakes on purpose, taking risks, and trying new things. It's just a matter of considering simple questions like

"What if?"

"What else?

Try something new! It doesn't have to be related to yarn. Try a new recipe or learn another craft. You don't have to be good at it or ever do it again. You can even buy yourself a coloring book and some crayons!

WE ARE ALL CREATIVE

As impossible as it may sound, it's true. Creativity is a process, and with practice it becomes as familiar as adding numbers or reading. People say, "I'm not creative," "I could never do that," or "How did you think of that?" There's no big secret. There are steps you can take to find and develop your own creativity, and then it's just a matter of practice. And creative knitting makes practice fun!

I really want you to read the following sentence and just sit with it for a moment.

Everyone is creative.

The biggest problem is reading that sentence and immediately reacting to it. Fear is a creativity killer. "No" is everywhere. From the time you're little, you're told to get good grades and that failure is not an option. It is! One wrong turn can lead to a whole new adventure. I had a painting teacher whose motto was "Dare to be lousy!" I'm giving you permission right now to make all the mistakes you want, and it'll be just fine.

The misconception I hear and see most is that creativity is intangible, a gift you're either born with or you're not. Creativity is no more a mystery than any other learned process. To get good at anything, you have to practice. Once you've been given the tools and invested the time, it's yours forever. Practice regularly and you'll start seeing things from a new perspective. You'll create new habits, look at the world differently, and find inspiration in simple things.

We all have a constant inner dialogue. For years I thought I needed to stop mine. Now I know it's always going to be there—but I can choose the content. Picture a big balloon filled with helium. The string of the balloon is tied to a small basket. When the thought "I'm not good enough" or "I can't do this" pops up, imagine yourself writing it on a piece of paper, sticking it in the basket, and watching the balloon float away. You may send up lots of balloons—and that's just fine!

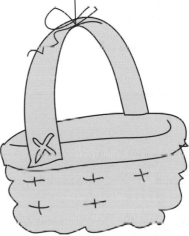

Maybe you find the thought of creative knitting intimidating. The idea of coming up with something out of nothing—of picking colors and deciding what to make—can be overwhelming. I understand that. Rules and instructions can be comfortable. Following a well-thought-out pattern and admiring the finished result has its own reward. But creative knitting has structure too. Once you learn the steps, you'll use them like an outline to explore different parts of your work one step at a time. It's too much to try and see the whole picture at once—we're going to break it into manageable parts.

We are exposed to an overwhelming amount of stimuli. Words and pictures fly at us and sounds bombard our ears. Creativity involves taking it all in and finding new ways to express it. It's like we're filters: stuff comes in, we process it, and we create something new. All of your experiences, sounds, sights, tastes, and smells are inspiration from which new ideas spring. And spring they do! Now you get to harness and combine them in different ways, and let others see how you interpret your own rich inner world.

Science keeps finding out more about how our brains work. They say that we process, understand, and remember in different parts of our brain—there's not one central memory bank. As we scan the world around us we label things, but our senses also form representations and memories that are stored in different ways. A large part of the creative process is allowing yourself to access memories that aren't stored as words. Sometimes it's a feeling or a vague memory. There's an expression I love: the mash-up. I saw it first on the tv show Glee, where it referred to the idea of taking 2 songs that have something in common and creating a new song that sounds familiar but has its own point of view. Creative knitting is another kind of mash-up. Some simple thing can spark an idea. I take a walk with my old lady dog, watch her romp through the purple petals that rain down from the Jacaranda trees onto the freshly mowed grass, and can't wait to get home to dive into my purple and green yarns. Or I go to a store and find myself distracted by the carpeting pattern. It all finds a way into my knitting.

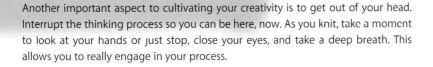

Another important aspect to cultivating your creativity is to get out of your head. Interrupt the thinking process so you can be here, now. As you knit, take a moment to look at your hands or just stop, close your eyes, and take a deep breath. This allows you to really engage in your process.

The word "creative" conjures up thoughts of "original." Honest artists will tell you that nothing is original. Everything is something else, transformed.

Let's do an exercise. Think about your favorite toy or game when you were little. Remember what you loved about it — where you were, who you were with… or were you alone? What was around you? Was it quiet, or noisy?

Go there for a moment. Close your eyes and picture yourself there. Recall what you loved about it.

While you played, you probably weren't thinking, "I'm really not very good at this," "I should stop, I don't know what I'm doing," or "Someone may tell me I'm doing it wrong or say I'm silly." Were you? Didn't think so.

Now that you have a strong sense of what it was to just play, I want you to tuck that feeling away and as you play with your yarn, I want you to revisit that feeling.

Returning to a place of play brings up all kinds of possibilities. You don't have to know what you're going to do. You just have to let yourself do it.

TOOLS FOR CREATIVITY

I collect pictures. Lots of pictures. Some are sweaters from catalogs and magazines, but most are just pictures that make me smile. Something resonates — maybe the colors or the pattern. Create your own collection — whether virtual or physical — and save the interesting images you come across. Mine are in a folder called "Inspiration." Often, before I start thinking about a design, I flip through my Inspiration folder until something catches my eye. I put it aside, then look for stitch patterns or think about techniques that remind me of elements from that image. A great way to pick colors for a project is to look at landscapes or graphic designs, create a palette, then find yarns to match.

Go shopping! Look at the construction of garments, and take notes. I've bought sweaters for their shapes and reverse engineered them by measuring the fronts, backs, and sleeves, then turned them into my own creations.

Make yourself files on your computer for cardigans, jackets, and pullovers, and whenever you come across an ad or picture of one you like, save it to your files. Before you begin a project, take time to just look at pictures. The influence of all the different styles and shapes will be part of your mash-up.

Here's a liberating thought: What you create doesn't even have to be good.

ALL creative expression is valid.

As you explore different possibilities, it will be important to allow yourself to try something without making any judgment about it after it's done. Remember, we are conditioned to judge and grade ourselves immediately, and it's really a matter of practice to allow ourselves to let go and just play, like we did when we were kids.

We look at most things very literally. A chair is just a chair. A good exercise to help train you to see things abstractly is the reverse-paper-doll method. When you played with paper dolls, you cut out the clothes and placed them over each other. We're going to do just the opposite. Take this picture of a T-shirt, make a copy of it on sturdy white paper and, using an X-ACTO knife, cut out the shape so you have a T-shirt-shaped window. Grab your scrap file or any magazine sitting around and randomly place the window over a picture. Now turn it upside down. Check out the shapes and colors in the window. Is there a flow to the direction of the lines? Is there an overall coloration? How about accent colors? Squint a little bit and see if it changes. Pick another picture and try it again. Isolating an area within a picture creates an abstract image that you can look at as inspiration.

Most importantly, make time every day to cultivate these new habits. Most only take a few minutes. Notice where you are, look at the stuff around you, check out what you're thinking about, and take mental notes of what you experience. No more than that, done on a daily basis, and inspiration will flow in no time.

Having T-shirt windows of different sizes can help you isolate small, non-representational elements.

WHAT IS CREATIVE KNITTING?

I like functional art. I love making things I can wear and use. I especially love to knit something specific, like a cardigan, without knowing how it's going to turn out. It morphs and evolves into a total surprise. There's nothing like staring at something you've finished and wondering where it came from! Just know that it didn't spring out of nowhere. When I analyze the colors and stitches, I see direct influences from something that caught my eye or from a technique I'm exploring. All that, combined with experience acquired through hours of knitting, helps me explore and play with an ever-growing toolbox.

The idea of the toolbox is a good way to understand the essentials you need to take on your own creative journey. The more skills you develop, the more tools you have for translating your vision. The more tools you have, the more inspiration will naturally flow through your fingers. I find it essential to keep learning new techniques. I take classes, read books, watch videos, and check out online forums. Your vision is a mash-up of all the things you've ever been exposed to. Creativity is not about reinventing the wheel—it's about transforming that wheel by combining it with something else. It's a pink wheel with purple polka dots that becomes a chair.

Here's another liberating idea—creative knitting doesn't have to have a purpose. It's nice to have a sweater at the end of your knitting, but there's value in knitting for the sake of knitting. I love to swatch. I swatch to try new techniques or stitch patterns, or just to see what a color combination looks like. I love making cables but don't have an opportunity to wear heavy sweaters, so sometimes I just knit a square with an interesting Celtic knot. You'll see later that there are lots of ways to incorporate swatches into Crazy Quilt and Freeform knitting.

I save small lengths in plastic bags so they're easy to grab, then put the swatches in those bags, they're little surprises that can inspire all sorts of fun. You can learn techniques by just doing a swatch rather than a whole project. Find a pattern with an interesting technique? Save the instructions with a swatch so you can remind yourself how to do it later. Try all kinds of techniques, even the ones you don't think you'll ever use—certainly not for an entire garment. Try them for a small section; try them in different yarns. Techniques can totally change character with a simple change of yarn.

Many of the tools used in other crafts are very handy for creative knitting. Quilting tools are especially helpful, such as a rotary cutter and mat for template cutting and acrylic rulers for drawing long, straight lines. Quilters also use special triangle rulers marked with lines at various angles that make sketching a specific triangular shape onto a template a breeze. I use the 30°, 45°, and 60° triangle rulers.

If you had to pick one word to describe them, what would it be? What's the overall feeling you get from them? Can you think of a song that reminds you of that feeling? What colors remind you of the experience? By doing the 3-things game regularly, you begin to see the mashups in seemingly unrelated things.

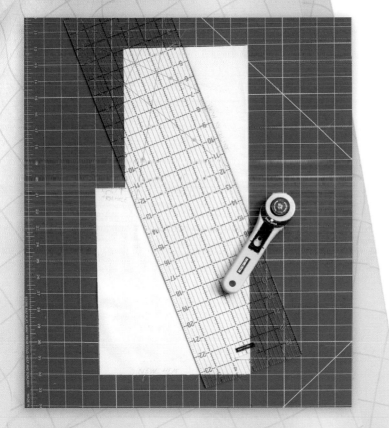

WHERE DO I START?

For a good traveling experience, having a map or GPS makes the ride smoother. Think of me as your tour guide. There's method to my madness, and a specific route to ensure an enjoyable and successful creative adventure. Along the way I suggest a few Alternate Routes, and you may find other roads you'd rather take. The creative approach is very flexible and you can change it to suit your style. Some of us are very structured explorers and like to plan everything out in advance—all routes are highlighted on maps and every stop along the way is indicated; measurements are made and calculations are done in advance. Other free-spirited adventurers delight in having no plan—changing directions frequently, and making spontaneous decisions en route. With a few basic tools and maps to start with, you can proceed as you like, adjusting your approach along the way.

WHAT TOOLS WILL I NEED?

The tools you'll need are the same basic tools needed for all knitting. I use a set of interchangeable needles with multiple lengths of cords, since I may use the same size tips in different areas but may also need to shorten or lengthen the cords as I knit. I also use double-pointed needles with stoppers on the ends as short needles for smaller areas of knitting—smaller means more portable. If you are selecting your own yarns or modifying the designs as you wish, you will need colored pencils that approximate your yarn colors. Grab a ruler and tape measure, a pencil with an eraser, some stitch markers, a yarn needle, and a crochet hook, and you'll be all set to go.

If you are venturing out on your own, you may also want a good library of stitch dictionaries. And if you're creating a template, you'll need fabric. There are so many advantages to the template-based approach that I really encourage you to try it. It's worth the effort, and once you make one garment template you can use it again and again, knowing whatever you make will fitr.

Make sure you have a comfortable place to sit, lots of light, and you might want to have a bar of chocolate or glass of wine handy—that always makes my expedition happier!

MASTER TEMPLATES: the 1, 2, 3

1
Choose your size

2
Enlarge to life-size on fabric: Pellon or muslin

3
Make any style changes to the life-size template

I find that simple geometric shapes are easy to work and the most flexible for creative knitting. You'll find the Master Templates on page 126 can be divided into panels or geometric shapes and filled in with any techniques and worked in any direction.

All you need to do is knit to fill in the templates knowing that, once the fabric is made, the pieces will come together easily. You will find simple custom-fitting options on page 127.

For most of the sweaters in this book, the first thing I recommend is that you create a life-size template. The Master Template is included for 6 sizes: 32", 36", 40", 44", 48", and 52". Choose your size, based on your bust measurement plus ease and enlarge the pieces to a life-size fabric template. The most direct route is to use Pellon Tru-Grid, available in fabric or craft stores or online, this sheer yet strong non-woven fabric has a 1" square grid printed on one side.

You may come to love knitting to a template and use it for all your knitting as I do. Just be aware that to make templates from other schematics, use the measurements to scale it up; do not trust that a photocopy enlargement will be to the correct proportions.

Templates

It makes sense that what you need for template-based creative knitting is a template—one that is your size, your life-size—and you need it in a material that you can "try on," draw on, and steam on. Simply shaped and easily adjustable, this template helps you focus on the creative parts of a garment, without worrying about the fit.

Templates are schematic pieces enlarged to life size. Use one, and you're free to change your mind and redirect your course at any time while you're knitting. Once the overall template shape is established and you know how the finished garment will fit, there are infinite ways to fill it in. Pick one overall technique or combine as many as you want. The template gives you guidelines to follow, but there are no set rules for how the journey has to progress. The true reward to this approach is knowing that your garment will fit, before you finish it!

In general, a template is cut out, tried on, then altered if necessary. Once the fit is established, the template is filled in with knitting all the way to the edges.

Unlike standard pattern knitting, where each piece is started at one end and worked to the other, you're free to fill in the template by starting wherever you'd like and knitting in any direction.

You can work on several parts of a garment at the same time, which can help you make decisions about how you want to knit the rest of the garment. You are free to change your mind at any time and to use different techniques, yarns, and colors.

Often you can move the knitted pieces around as you like. The only rule is that the entire template must be covered. Think of the template as a frame for a jigsaw puzzle; it is done when the entire frame is filled in without any overlaps or gaps.

And you don't need a new template for each sweater you make based on this master. It holds up and is easy to adjust for a V-neck, a shorter body, or other style and fit variations. Just fold or slash and baste in the change.

To have a clean canvas for a different design panel, cut a new template for just that section and mark your design lines on it.

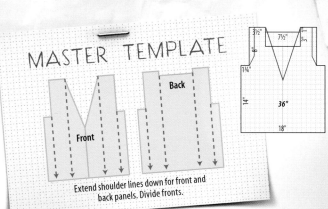

MASTER TEMPLATE

Front

Back

3½"   7½"   3"
8"
1¾"
14"   36"
18"

Extend shoulder lines down for front and back panels. Divide fronts.

Most projects use this master template as a starting point. The instructions may ask you to modify its shape as shown by a small icon.

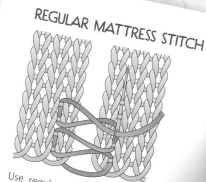

REGULAR MATTRESS STITCH

Use regular mattress stitch for structural garment seams—shoulders, sides, underarms.

Using Pellon for life-size templates

In the past I have used various methods for making a life-size template — marking measurements directly on muslin, making a paper enlargement at a copy shop to as a pattern for cutting the muslin, even scanning in my small gridded sketch before enlarging it on the computer and tiling to print — now I make a Pellon template. Available in most fabric stores or online, this sheer yet strong polyester fabric has a one-inch square grid printed on one side.

Transferring one of the mini master templates found on page 127 onto the Pellon is very easy. Lay the Pellon flat, making sure you have enough width and length for the life-size pattern piece. With a pencil, mark the center vertical grid line 1" from the bottom edge. Counting out to the right and left of this line, mark the width for the bottom of the piece. Complete the outline by counting and marking the number of squares that correspond to the inches from the small schematic. The mini master templates provided in this book are already gridded, so you can just count the squares from the small schematic and outline the same number of squares on the 1" grid.

Once you've placed all these points, use a fine, red, permanent marker and long ruler to connect the dots and write the measurements inside the lines for easy reference. Cut out the Pellon pieces along the lines. To check the fit, you can pin at the seams with as little seam allowance as possible and try them on. Start with just the front and back, leaving one side seam open for a pullover. Since the fabric does not have the give that a knit does, pin the sleeve together at the underarm and try it on separately. Make any adjustments to the template before starting your knitting.

The project determines whether I use muslin or Pellon. If I'm planning a Crazy Quilt or Freeform piece where I may need to draw out a number of lines and angles, I want a blank canvas and use muslin. If not, it's really nice to have the gridlines for easy steaming and measuring as I knit. Try both and see which you prefer. If I do want to use muslin, the Pellon can be used as a pattern for cutting out the muslin pieces.

Steam blocking works wonderfully, and the Pellon holds up as well as fabric with the steam-as-you-go method. When you iron out creases, place a piece of cotton fabric over the Pellon and avoid direct contact with the iron.

So buy a couple of yards of Tru-Grid and a fine, waterproof marker or 2 and go 100% — go direct to Pellon.

Unlike structural seams, Modified Mattress Stitch joins and assembles the fabric itself and is important to the drape of the garment. The goal of the modified stitch is to join pieces with as little bulk as possible, so think of it as fabric assembly rather than as seams. Structural seams are made with regular mattress stitch.

MODIFIED MATTRESS STITCH

Stockinette join
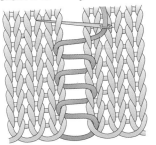

Garter-stitch join
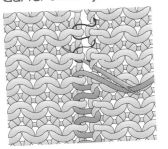

Stitch-to-row join
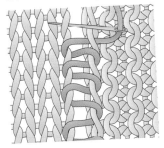

Use Modified Mattress Stitch for joins when assembling the fabric.

Determine which size templates from this book or any other pattern schematics will fit you best.

Start with the bust measurement, then check the width around the hemline. If the hip is larger, page 127 includes directions for adding flare to the side panels — this avoids using a larger size to accommodate wider hips.

Compare your back bust and front bust measurements; you may need a smaller size in back than in front. That may be why a specific size pattern, although the right overall measurement for you, is often too loose in back and too tight in front.

A template makes it so easy to combine sizes: I use a small back and medium front. Once I transfer the paper template to the fabric, I adjust the armholes to match the larger size. I also use the sleeves for the larger size so they fit the adjusted armhole. It is possible to use 2 sizes without a template, too. By doing a little math, you can adjust a pattern between sizes and rewrite the instructions, but it's much easier to just make a template!

Considering construction

Now that the template is complete there are many routes to take to the finished garment. You can choose a stitch pattern for the whole garment or break it into sections, using different techniques and stitches for each section. Feel free to mix and match techniques! Since the finished garments will be washed with care, you're free to mix fiber content along with color, technique, and texture, as long as the yarn weights are consistent. Decide the weight of the overall yarn (fingering, sport, DK, worsted) and stick to that weight for all of the yarns you use.

Altering the template

You may find your life-size fabric template needs alteration for a perfect fit. A template can be used over and over, so it's worth taking the time to get it right. Having a helper is the best way, and if it's a knitting buddy you can work on 2 templates at the same time — one for each! Otherwise, look for an adjustable dress form, or check YouTube or Google "duct tape dress form" for instructions on how to make one.

TOO SMALL   If there's not enough fabric and the fit is too tight, you can cut additional strips of Pellon to insert at each side, or at the front edges if it's a cardigan. Most of the time you'll want to divide the area needed between the right and left sides. Cut strips to that size, then tape them onto the template. We'll smooth any bumps and make sure the lines are even in the next phase. Right now, you just need to know how much fabric to add.

TOO LARGE   If there's too much fabric, pinch the excess fabric and pin, adjusting both the left and right sides evenly. It's easiest to have help with this process.

SLEEVES AND ARMHOLES   Once the body of the garment fits, check the sleeves. Any adjustments made to the armholes need to have corresponding changes made to the sleeves. First, make sure the armhole is comfortable and fits well, then adjust the sleeve measurements accordingly. During the next step, compare the armhole to the sleeve and redraw if necessary (for example, an 8-inch armhole needs 16-inches of sleeve width).

Redrawing the template

After pinning the excess or adding more fabric during fitting, it's time to redraw the lines. Fold the fabric template in half on the center fold line and smooth out any bubbles from pins or tape. If you are removing fabric, redraw the lines on one side of the template. Cut the new lines for both left and right sides at the same time, to ensure that both halves are the same. If lots of alterations have been made to any pattern piece, or if you've inserted more fabric, you will want to recut a final template for each pattern piece needed. If you recut pieces, go ahead and try them on again.

Make sure to draw lines on the template for areas that will be reserved for button bands, hem lines, cuffs, and edgings, so they won't be factored into the initial measuring for the knitting of each section. Also check the hem length and make sure the fronts and backs are even, unless you are building in extra for more coverage.

Once the lines are redrawn to the right measurements, cut each piece to the edge of the final lines. I like to use a rotary cutter rather than scissors. Check the quilting department of your local craft or fabric store for a rotary cutter, cutting mat, and Plexiglas ruler. These tools cut straight lines much more accurately than scissors. Now, using clips or tape, connect the fabric at the seams, matching the very edges of the fabric.

Template library

Write the name of each pattern piece on each template piece. I like to store them in 8" × 10" envelopes — like traditional sewing patterns — to keep them organized and easily accessible. I'll write a small description on the front of the envelope so I can easily refer back to that template. I've used the same template multiple times for different designs, knowing that whatever I make will fit just like the other garment I made from the same template. It's a beautiful thing.

Rearranging templates

The templates can be rearranged in a number of different ways, depending on how you'd like to fill them in. The schematic used in Southwestern Splendor (A), indicates two fronts, a back, and two sleeves, all worked separately. Within that layout, further divisions into panels can be made any way you'd like.

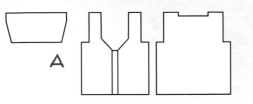

In B, the pieces have been rearranged so there are no shoulder seams, allowing a pattern or design element to travel from the front, over the shoulders, and onto the back. In Freeform or Crazy Quilt knitting, since the pieces are smaller and usually worked on the bias, seams across the shoulders aren't as necessary for stability. Sleeves can be knit separately and sewn into the armholes as shown on the left, or can be worked in one piece with the garment as shown on the right. The advantage to the layout on the right is that the patterning, motifs, etc., can flow over the entire garment, with no breaks for seams at the shoulders or armholes.

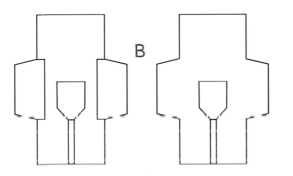

C eliminates the sides seams so patterning can flow around the entire the garment, offering possibilities for dividing into panels, motifs, etc., that cross from one side to the other without interruption.

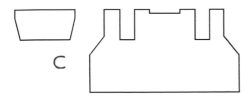

Any schematic can be rearranged to suit your design. An easy way to decide how you'd like to construct any garment is to take the small schematic printed in a book or magazine, photocopy it, cut it out, and start exploring options for alternate constructions.

Template options

SIDE PANELS AND SET-IN SLEEVES

Something to consider when deciding on how to divide a template into panels is how you want to finish the piece. There are advantages to each approach, but considerations as well.

Template D shows the side panels attached to the front and back separately, to be finished with side seams. This is commonly used with simple stitch patterns like garter stitch, garter ridges, or a simple 2- to 4-stitch repeat.

Template E shows a one-piece side panel, picked up from the fronts and seamed to the back. The panel could also be knit separately and seamed to both the front and back. Either way, with this approach there is no interruption at the side seam when a more complicated stitch pattern such as a lace panel is used.

FINISHING
The finishing for each of these is slightly different, and something to consider.

Flat assembly
Side panels that are seamed at the side, as in Template D, are laid flat to set in the sleeve.

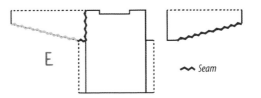

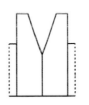

Set-in assembly
For one-piece side panels, as in Template E, the panels are picked up and/or seamed to the body first, then the sleeves are seamed and set into the armhole. For details on both approaches to seaming, see page 119.

~~~ Seam

Now that the template is complete, there are many routes to a finished garment. You can choose a stitch pattern for the whole garment, or break it into sections and use different stitches for each. Feel free to mix and match techniques, too.

COLOR You know what you want to make — the next step is to pick the colors. There are lots of ideas about color theory, but I believe it's more important to pick what you love and what you'll wear. I know I'll wear a purple and green sweater again and again.

A variegated yarn or a yarn that has a long repeat is a great way to venture outside your comfort range. Someone has already done the color selection, so you can just pick a combination you love. The difference between variegated and long repeat is the length before one color changes to a new color—anywhere from 2–3 inches to about 8–10 inches for a varigated, and from 5–10 yards to way longer for a long repeat. With a long repeat you can work directly from the ball for self-striping. Or you can divide each ball into smaller balls of individual colors to use as you'd like — I call this **controlling the color**. Since each ball has 2 ends, you have a variety of starting points from just a couple of balls of yarn.

YARN It's time to pick yarns. First, consider use and drape. Do you want a heavy or a light garment? Something to wear over other clothing? What type of fiber are you interested in using? Because this type of knitting tends to use more than one yarn in a piece, you may be able to mix yarns, but for the best drape they should be about the same weight. I've made suggestions for the designs in this book, but substituting a different fiber or weight is always an option.

To determine how much yarn you'll need to complete the sweater, refer to the yardage estimates on page 125. Allow extra if you combine yarns or colors — especially when controlling the color in a long-repeat yarn. There may be a color that you want to control right out of the sweater!

If you are using multiple balls of different fibers or colors, place all the yarns together on a table to see if they work together. Check the yarn weights — if one you love is too thin, you can try doubling it. Remove any colors or fibers that don't work. Specialty and novelty yarns can be added for accent areas. Make sure you're happy with the way all the yarns look together.

SKETCHING When creating a new design, I sketch ideas onto a small version of the schematic using colored pencils that match my yarns.

Small schematics of each design are provided. You can use them to modify one of the book's designs or to create your own. Copy your mini template and have fun with it. You don't need to draw — just use a pencil to indicate the separate knitted pieces, then color in areas to match your yarn selection. Once you're happy, transfer the style lines to the full-size fabric template. If you're preplanning, you'll want to have all of the specific areas drawn onto the muslin. Divide areas into measurements close to an inch or a half inch, for easy calculations later. Lay balls of yarn in different areas to see how they'll work together, then tape snippets of yarn to help you remember.

SWATCHING Swatching is normally done to match a specific gauge indicated in a pattern. Here, your swatches usually do not need to match a specific stitch or row count. Instead, they are test runs to determine the drape and density you want for your fabric.

Once you've chosen the needle size you like best, it's time to play with stitch patterns! Make yourself a mini stitch/technique library, either paper or digital. I copy my favorite stitch patterns onto 3 × 5 index cards for easy access. Start with the needles you think you'd use for the yarn of your choice.

This is a great time to break out those interchangeable needles! Cast on and begin a swatch, working an inch of garter, and an inch of stockinette, then try it with needles 1 size up or down. Check to see how the fabric feels. I often swatch with 3 different sizes to get a feel for the possibilities of the fabric. Keep notes on a tag you'll attach to the swatch indicating the yarn, color, and needle sizes. Your tagged swatches create a great resource library you can return to for future projects! Block the swatch the same way you will block the garment, and allow it to sit undisturbed for a few hours to make sure the fabric has completely settled before the gauge is counted. I often knit a bunch of swatches and block right before bed so they'll be ready to choose from in the morning. If you're using different yarns within the same piece, you'll want to knit swatches with each and try to approximate a similar drape and density, even if it means using a different needle size for each yarn. Even though most garments will be knit in joined sections, their fabrics should be consistent in density for a good overall drape.

Now try all kinds of stitches and techniques. This is a great time to try out a technique you know or one that you love but would not necessarily use for an entire sweater. Most importantly, pick techniques you enjoy. Grab your stitch guides and your yarn and needles, and cast on 28: 2 on each end for borders and 24 in the middle. 24 is a magical number for pattern repeats, evenly divisible by 2, 3, 4, 6, 8, and 12. In general, the flow of patterns works best when the pattern repeats are divisible by common numbers so they can line up over each other. A repeat of 7 won't look great over a repeat of 6, but a repeat of 3 or 12 would.

BLOCKING Blocking the swatches is essential. You need to know how large the fabric will be and how the fabric will feel. Until a fabric is blocked, you don't really know how it will behave. After binding off, lay the swatch out on an ironing or blocking board, smooth with your hand, and pin the corners with T-pins without stretching the fabric. Hover the steam iron or steamer over the fabric, give it a few good shots of steam, then take the steamer away. With your fingers, press the edges of the fabric flat. Make sure the piece is lying the way you want the final fabric to be, then hit it with another shot or two of steam, and allow to dry. Some fabrics, especially stockinette, tend to roll at the edges. Turn the swatch over and steam just the edges, then use your fingers to press them flat. At this point, you can decide which needle size you want to use for the garment, by holding the swatch in your hands and allowing it to hang vertically. It really is that simple.

a journey into creativity →→→ 19

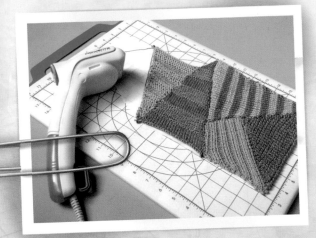

Let's get going!

If you're following the directions for a specific garment, you're ready to get started. If you're interested in exploring different possibilities using the same templates but with different yarns, techniques, or needle sizes, some simple math may be necessary. It's not scary math since all you're really doing is measuring the cast-on edge for each area.

Gauge

When you explore different stitch patterns than those used in a pattern, you don't need to match a *specific* gauge, but you need *your* gauge to know how many stitches will fit the template. Once you've picked the swatches you like best, measure how many stitches fit into one inch. I like to measure across 4 inches and divide by 4 for a more accurate count. Record this stitch gauge on a swatch tag or in project notes. Since I use many of the same yarns and needles over and over for different projects, I have a swatch collection already tagged with gauge information. Often I use the same basic gauge for similar stitches using yarns of the same weight without having to knit a new swatch — just steam to the template and adjust needle size if needed.

Graphic patterns: the overview

Now it's time to decide how you want to approach your expedition. My favorite method is to draw areas onto the template, but to decide after I complete one section which stitch to use for the next. You can plan the entire journey beforehand or make decisions along the way. In either case, you'll create a graphic pattern — your actual map — which indicates the cast-on count, knitting directions, and chosen stitch patterns. Gather a copy of your small schematic with lines delineating each area to knit, your life-size template with those lines drawn onto the fabric, a ruler, and your gauge swatches.

For each area that starts with more than 3 stitches, measure the edge where you want to cast on, remembering that you're free to knit side-to-side or top-to-bottom. Write that number on your small template with an arrow indicating the knitting direction. Multiply your stitch gauge by the inches to be cast on.

Steam as you go

As you knit, it's crucial that you check your progress against the template. After a few inches, place the knitting over the template to see how it fits and how many more rows are needed.

Pin the corners of the cast-on edge to that line on the template and steam lightly to relax the knitting. If the piece is too wide or too narrow, you'll need to start over, adjusting the number of cast-on stitches to fit. Knit to fill the area.

As you knit, you'll steam the garment pieces right onto the template to make sure they fit. After binding off, pin the corners of each piece, steam a little at a time, and use your fingers to straighten edges to the lines within the template. Since steaming relaxes the fabric, it grows slightly, so knit each section to just within the lines drawn on the template. Allow the fabric to settle naturally rather than stretching it. If the piece is too small or too large, reknit it rather than forcing it to fit.

Since I'm a sofa-based crafter and like to have everything within reach, I use a small blocking board, available in quilting departments, along with a hand steamer. Swatches and many of the knitted pieces are small, so I can steam as I go on the board right in my lap. For pieces too large to block on the small board, I use an ironing board or a larger blocking board. Most importantly, I make sure the knitted pieces fill in the template exactly; they should not fall short or overlap the template edges.

As each area is completed, it's joined to an adjacent area with Modified Mattress Stitch as shown on page 15. All of the joins within the front, back, and sleeve fabrics are done before final seaming and finishing. I like to leave long tails at the bind-off to use for this.

The road ahead

More than anything else, I don't want you to be a slave to instructions — even *my* instructions. Although I may give complete directions for techniques and patterns, I don't expect or even encourage you to follow them to a T. There is no *right* way to knit. Everyone holds the yarn and tosses or picks it their own way. If *you* are happy with the resulting fabric, the way you made it is as valid as any other.

Think of the directions in this book as your starting point, with many decisions that can be made along the way. Just feel free to recalibrate frequently, as my GPS does.

Notes

• *Make sure to steam the swatch, just as you'll steam the garment before measuring. Once the swatch is dry, measure carefully and record the gauge.*

• *Always round to the nearest half inch.*

• *Measure over 4 inches and divide by 4 for gauge.*

• *Larger pieces of the final garment will relax, so the gauge may change as you knit. Always check the gauge as you knit by steaming lightly every few inches.*

Mod Knitting

Strips, modules, & angles

The first and easiest approach to creative knitting uses blocks: squares, rectangles, and strips. You can simply proceed from a swatch and work a section, work several separate swatches and put them together, or pick up stitches and work out from the first swatch in any direction to build your fabric.

This is an ideal time to play with stitch dictionaries! Swatch like crazy to see which fabrics you like best and how they look next to each other. You'll soon find that some stitches and yarns work well together, while others do not! Feel free to experiment with color and even yarn combinations on your way to your final decisions.

After swatching, note the gauge — the number of stitches and rows in 1" — of the patterns you chose. You will find slight gauge differences using the same needle size between stockinette, garter, rib, stranded colorwork, lace, and cables.

Next, divide a mini template with horizontal and vertical lines. Be conscious of the lines that flow along, perpendicular to, or parallel with the construction lines in a garment — shoulder edge, armhole, side of neck, and center front or back.

Once you are happy with the placement of the lines and strips, draw them onto your life-size template. This is the place to note the direction in which you will knit each strip, along with the color, yarn, and/or stitch pattern for each. Note the measurements for each section. These numbers will soon be converted into stitch and row counts, but it's probably best to wait until you arrive at that section — your plans may change, and that's what creativity is all about, after all!

As you pick a stitch pattern, consider how many repeats fit into the area. Centering full repeats usually makes for a very successful fabric. Make sure to steam as you knit to make sure the strip fits the template or schematic perfectly. No seam allowance is needed, since you'll join each section with Modified Mattress Stitch. As you knit, remember to stop short of the desired length — you can always add a few rows after steaming. As each section is knit, join it to the adjacent areas.

There are a couple of patterns included to get you started. Here, the size, pattern, color, and stitch choices have already been made, but feel free to change it up however you like. Small refinements may be all it takes to create your own perfect original design.

Another approach to creative knitting is working in the modular style. Many small modules are worked separately and then assembled, or picked up and knit as you go to form larger garment pieces.

Sketches get my creativity going, and I can arrive at a fairly complete plan well before I cast on my first stitch. And you don't need to be an artist—just start with a mini template of the garment you like. Decide which pieces will be modular—maybe just the center front as in Magical Milestones, page 46, or Star Traveler, page 47, in which the center sections are broken into grids of equal-sized squares.

Create a grid for that section, make copies, and then color in your ideas, mixing colors to match the yarns you plan to use. Make as many configurations as you like until you arrive at your favorite. You might even cut out motifs from colored paper and arrange them like a mosaic or puzzle. Some ideas come together right away, while others take time—enjoy that process.

It's almost time to knit!

I prefer to work in garter stitch. Two rows of garter (1 ridge) are essentially as tall as 1 stitch is wide, so making a square in garter is easy—it takes twice as many rows as stitches. Garter is invaluable for working bias fabric, since you can cast on 1 stitch, increase at the beginning of every row, and the edges will create a perfect right angle. Bind off for a half-square right triangle, or change color and decrease back down to 1 stitch to create a bias square made of 2 half-square triangles.

Once you have made the required decisions of yarns, colors, and placement, gauge and block size come into play. Measure each module and do the math to convert the size of each module into stitches and rows. Now start knitting!

My general approach is to pick up and knit off of an edge whenever possible, then use Modified Mattress Stitch as necessary. You will see this process in the patterns, but will develop the methods that best suit you. Remember, there are no rules for being creative—try something and see what happens!

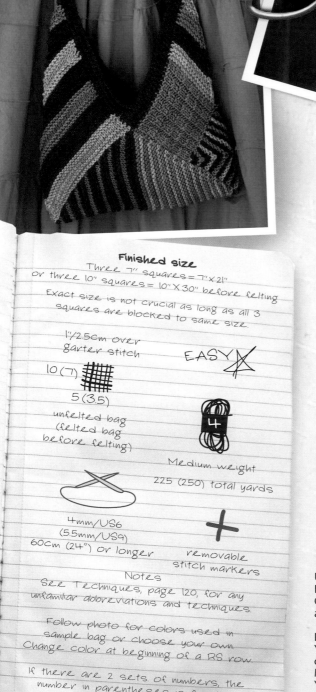

Rows 1 and 3 (RS) P1, **[k2, p1]** to end.
Row 2 K1, **[p2, k1]** to end.
Row 4 Knit.

```
4  ▢▢▢▢▢       ☐ Knit on RS, purl on WS
2  ▢▢▢▢▢  3    ▨ Purl on RS, knit on WS
         1
   └3-st┘
   repeat
```

MITERED SQUARE
Pick up stitches as directed. Mark center stitch.
RS rows Work to 1 stitch before marked stitch, S2KP2, work to end —2 stitches decreased.
WS rows Work even.
When 1 stitch remains, cut yarn and fasten off. Steam.

Finish your bag

Felted bag Felt in washing machine in hot water to desired size. Block.

Both bags Follow Steps 1–4 to fold and seam the bag. **Round 1** Join yarn to open edge, sc evenly around, sl st to join and AT THE SAME TIME, at top corners, (2 sc, ch 2, 2 sc) in same space; at bottom of Vs, sc 2 together. **Round 2** Ch 2, hdc in each sc, sl st to join and AT THE SAME TIME, at top corners, (2 hdc, ch 2, 2 hdc) in same space; at bottom of Vs, hdc 2 together. **Round 3** Ch 1, reverse sc in each hdc, sl st to join, cut yarn, weave in end.

Make shoulder strap in I-cord or Twisted Cord. Leave long tails at both ends. Bring each end of cord through ch-2 space at top corners, tie a large overhand knot at bottom of cord, and weave in tail to secure knot.

Unfelted bag: FIESTA YARNS Boomerang in colors 3915 Grape Skin, 3956 Goldenrod, and 3907 Carnation

Felted bag: BROWN SHEEP YARN Lamb's Pride Worsted in colors M171 Fresh Moss and M205 Grassy Knoll; CASCADE YARNS Casablanca in color 15 Southwest Desert

Finished size
Three 7" squares = 7" x 21"
or three 10" squares = 10" x 30" before felting

Exact size is not crucial as long as all 3 squares are blocked to same size.

1"/2.5cm over garter stitch

EASY

10 (7)
5 (3.5)
unfelted bag (felted bag before felting)

Medium weight
225 (250) total yards

4mm/US6
(5.5mm/US9)
60cm (24") or longer

removable stitch markers

Notes
See Techniques, page 120, for any unfamiliar abbreviations and techniques.

Follow photo for colors used in sample bag or choose your own. Change color at beginning of a RS row.

If there are 2 sets of numbers, the number in parentheses is for the felted bag.

Far East of EDEN

Make the squares

1 Diagonal square Cast on 1, kf&b&f—3 stitches. Working in garter stitch, kf&b at the beginning every row until sides measure 7 (10)", then k2tog at the end of every row until 1 stitch remains. Cut yarn and fasten off. Steam.

2 Mitered square Pick up and knit (PUK) 35 from left edge of Square 1, then cast on 36—71 stitches. Work Mitered Square in the following pattern: *Row 1* (WS) Knit 1 row. **[Knit 3 rows, purl 1 row, knit 4 rows, change color, knit 1 row]**.

3 4-patch square For each small square, begin as follows: PUK the number of stitches with RS facing and knit 1 WS row.

a PUK19 along opposite edge of Square 1 to center as shown in drawing. Work six 4-row repeats of Waffle Stitch. Bind off.

b PUK18 along left edge of 3a, PUK17 along edge of Square 1. Work Mitered Square in the following pattern: **[Knit 2 rows, change color, knit 1 row, purl 1 row, change color]**.

c PUK19 from edge of 3b. Work as for 3a.

d PUK17 from 3a then 18 from 3c. Work Mitered Square in the following pattern: **[Knit 8 rows, change color]**.

— Cast on
••••• Pick up and knit
→ Direction of work

The felted bag before felting. Here stitches for the mitered square are first cast on, then picked up. The 4-patch square builds off of the mitered square.

Alternate Route

Create the squares separately and sew them together to create 1 long rectangle.

FOLD THE BAG

1

With WS together, fold diagonally along center square.

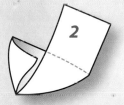

2

Fold left square diagonally so outer point touches front point of center block.

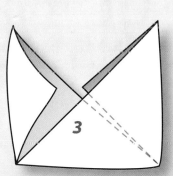

3

Flip bag over and fold remaining point in to meet point of center block.

4 Mattress stitch seam, flip bag over, and seam other side.

a journey into creativity →→→ 25

What a great little project bag!

A center strip of mitered squares is bordered by garter ridges and flanked with triangle panels, made using an intriguing technique. It's fast and fun to make.

The fold-over flap and button clasp keep all your goodies safe inside. The twisted cord combines all of the yarns used in the main piece. Any yarn can be used, since the final size isn't crucial.

Dancing diamonds

EASY +

Size
10" × 12"

10 [grid] 1"/2.5cm over
5 garter

[yarn]
4

4.5mm/US7
60cm (24") or longer

Medium weight
450 total yards as shown (50% each for A and B)

Notes
See Techniques, page 120, for unfamiliar abbreviations and techniques.

+

removable mark...
crochet hook
fusible fleece inter...
lining fabric an...
matching threa...
large button

MITERED SQUARE
Cast on and/or pick up and knit (PUK) stitches as directed. Mark center stitch with a removable marker. **Next row and all WS rows** Knit. **RS rows** Work to 1 stitch before marked stitch, S2KP2, work to end—2 stitches decreased. When 1 stitch remains, either cut yarn and fasten off or continue to next Miter.

1 Make 2 triangle panels
Vertical Triangle
With A, cast on 15 for first triangle in strip OR with RS facing, pick up and knit (PUK) 15 along top of diagonal triangle. **Row 1 and all WS rows** Knit. **Row 2 and all RS rows** Knit to last 2 stitches, k2tog. Work until 3 stitches remain. **Next RS row** SK2P; do not cut yarn.

Diagonal triangle
With RS facing and B, PUK21 along long edge of previous triangle. **All WS rows** Knit. **All RS rows** SSK, knit to last 2 stitches, k2tog. Work until 3 stitches remain. **Next RS row** SK2P, cut yarn, and pull through. Continue alternating vertical and diagonal triangles until panel measures 18" or desired length. Cut yarn and weave in ends. Steam to 3"×18". Make second panel and reverse colors: Work vertical triangles in B and diagonal triangles in A.

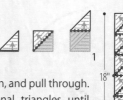

2 Add edging to each panel
With RS facing and A, PUK15 along left side of each diagonal triangle—90 stitches. Knit 1 row. Do not cut yarn. With B, knit 2 rows. Cut yarn. With A, knit 2 rows. Bind off. Repeat edging on edge of second panel.

3 Make miters along first panel
Miter A With B, cast on 14, and with RS of triangle panel facing, PUK15 along edging as shown. Work Mitered Square, changing colors as desired.
Miters B–F PUK14 from left edge of previous mitered square, PUK15 from edging. Work Mitered Square changing colors as desired.

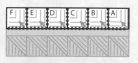

4 Assemble pieces
Mattress stitch edging of second triangle panel to edge of mitered squares.

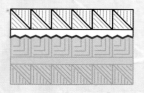

...ians → → →

5 Add side edging

With RS facing and A, PUK90 on each side of full panel and work edgings as in step 2, but do not bind off. Place stitches on hold. Fold pouch in half with RS together (making sure 45 stitches are on each side) and join sides with a 3-needle bind-off. Repeat on other side. Turn bag RS out.

6 Add top edging

With RS facing and A, and starting at seam at left edge, PUK108 around top edge (14 stitches across each panel, 3 in each edging, 1 in each seam), place marker, and join to work in the round. Work 5 rounds in garter (knit 1 round, purl 1 round). **Next round** K54, bind off 54. Do not cut yarn.

7 Work flap

Beginning with B and RS facing, work back and forth in garter stitch, changing color at beginning of every RS row. **All RS rows** Knit to last 3, k2tog, sl 1, **All WS rows** K1 tbl, knit to last 3, k2tog, sl 1. When 3 stitches remain, SK2P, cut yarn, and fasten off. With A, single crochet evenly along flap edge, making a large button-loop at the point.

Finish your bag

Finish Envelope style (page 115).

Strap

Make twisted cord and attach each end to each side at opening.

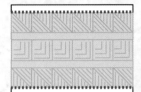

— Cast on
— Bind off
····· Pick up and knit
∿ Seam
→ Direction of work

Use a calculator, a phone app, or the web to find the square root!

Alternate Route

This modular technique can be used to make any size of square: Cast on any number you'd like for the starting triangle and decrease at the end of every RS row.

Take the number of stitches cast on for the triangle, multiply it by itself, then multiply the answer by 2. Find the square root of that number and round to the nearest odd number: This is the number of stitches to pick up along the diagonal edge of the vertical triangle. Make sure to pick up first and last stitches in it's corners.

Example: Cast on 15 for vertical triangle

$15 \times 15 = 225 \times 2 = 450$

Square root of $450 = 21$

Rounded to nearest odd number = 21, the number of stitches to pick up along the vertical triangle.

One Size: UNIVERSAL YARN Classic Shades in color 704 Reef (A); PRISM YARNS Symphony in color 112 (B)

Radiant rainbow

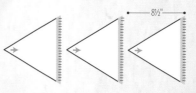

1 Make 60-degree triangles

Triangles 1, 2, and 3

With A, cast on 1, kf&b&f—3 stitches.

Rows 1, 2, and 4 Knit.

Row 3 Kf&b, knit to last stitch, kf&b — 2 stitches increased. Continue to increase at beginning and end every 4 rows until it measures 8½" from tip to center stitch on needle; note the number of stitches and garter ridges— approximately 39 stitches and 37 ridges. Knit 2 more rows. With B, work 4 rows in stockinette, place stitches on hold, and cut yarn, leaving a 24" tail.

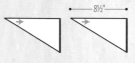

2 Make 30-degree triangles

Triangles 4 and 5

With A, cast on 1, kf&b — 2 stitches.

Rows 1, 2, and 4 Knit.

Row 3 Kf&b, knit to end — 1 stitch increased.

Mark increase edge, and increase on that edge only.

Continue to increase at the beginning every 4 rows until the same number of garter ridges have been worked as in the 60-degree triangle. Bind off.

CASCADE YARNS Souk in color 1 Rainbow (A) and Cascade 220® in color 8555 Black (B)

Front panel

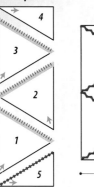

3 Join triangles

Arrange triangles as shown.

With B, pick up and knit (PUK) approximately 39 along angled edge of Triangle 5. Work 3 rows stockinette. Cut yarn, leaving a 24" tail.

With B, graft Triangles **1** and **5** together.

Place held stitches on needle and join remaining triangles as follows:

Graft **1** to **2**,

Graft **2** to **3**,

Graft **3** to **4**.

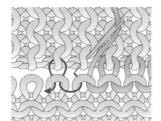

Graft live stitches to rows in garter stitch; match a stitch and a ridge (2 rows).

4 Make edging

Steam rectangle to 8½" × 22".

Borders With RS facing and B, PUK98 along long edge of rectangle. Work 3 rows in stockinette. Do not cut yarn.

Row 4 (RS) With A, **[k2, sl 2 wyib]** to last 2 stitches, k2.

Row 5 (WS) K2, **[sl 2 wyif, k2]** to end. Repeat last 2 rows. Work 4 rows in stockinette; place stitches on hold.

Repeat along opposite edge.

····· *Pick up and knit*
── *Bind off*
∿∿ *3-needle bind-off or graft*
⋮⋮⋮ *Stitches on hold*
→ *3 rows in stockinette in B*
→ *Direction of work*

Finish your bag

Finish tote-style (page 114). Fold bag in half with RS together (making sure 49 stitches are on each side) and join sides with 3-needle bind-off. Turn bag RS out and steam seams.

Straps

Buy ready made or, even better, find an old handbag at a thrift store and reuse the straps. Attach to the edge of the single crochet with an overcast stitch from the same yarn, then weave in ends.

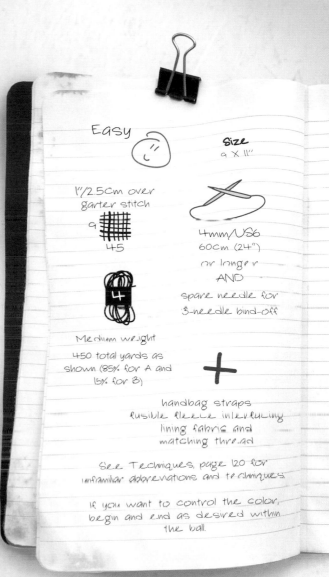

Easy

Size
9 × 11"

1"/2.5cm over garter stitch

9

45

Medium weight

450 total yards as shown (85% for A and 15% for B)

4mm/US6
60cm (24") or longer
AND
spare needle for 3-needle bind-off

handbag straps
fusible fleece interfacing
lining fabric and matching thread

See Techniques, page 120 for unfamiliar abbreviations and techniques.

If you want to control the color, begin and end as desired within the ball.

Block party cardi

Alternate Route

Sometimes you can change plans at the finishing stage. I avoided having to shape the V-neck while knitting lace by starting the neck decreases higher. When working the front band, I realized that the V should be lower and simply moved the buttons and buttonholes down. It worked!

MASTER TEMPLATE

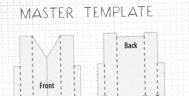

Shorten body 5".

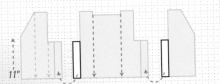

Measure 11" up to start V-neck. Draw a line from that point to shoulder.

Extend style lines down from the shoulder for left front and back strips. Divide fronts. Add right front underarm panel to right back and left back underarm panel to left front.

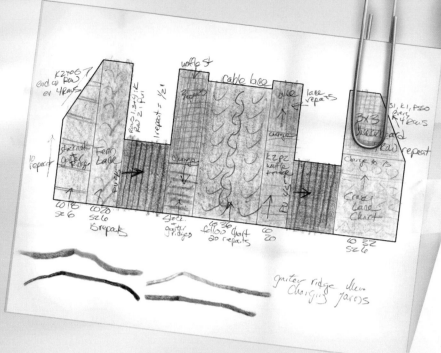

Point of interest

Some laces look almost the same, whether worked from the top down or from the bottom up. This is the case with Chart VII on page 34. An easy way to make sure that you don't have a partial 16-row repeat at the shoulder? Work the right back strip from the shoulder down!

Block Party started its excursion with the idea of using one continuous template to make the best use of an overall space. The plan was to divide the entire body into vertical panels that would be worked in different directions, each with a different stitch pattern. Since each panel is knit separately at its own gauge, I knew I could include lace along with more solid stitch patterns — easy!

I usually start with an idea for the overall shape of my garment, and then set out to find a yarn that will work best for the type of drape I want to achieve. I found a yarn I adore for its silky, warm, and cuddly quality, and in one of my favorite colors. I decided to do a monochromatic color scheme, so I picked several blues that worked well together.

A sketch is next, so I printed out a copy of my template and drew right onto it to see how I wanted to divide the areas, using colored pencils to approximate the colors I'd use in each section. I transferred the dividing lines to the life-size template, then looked for stitch patterns that worked well together, looking at them straight on, sideways, and upside down to see how they changed just by changing the direction of knitting. On the sketch, I noted the stitch to use for each panel along with its orientation.

The beauty of this approach is that you are free to knit the sections in the order you like, deciding as you knit how you want to join the next section, either by picking up from an edge or by knitting an individual piece and stitching it on. In either case, when you're done with the fabric, the seams are done, too!

Time to swatch. The suggested needle size was too loose so I moved down a couple of sizes, knit a square on 25 stitches (my usual cast-on for a swatch), then knit about 5 ridges in garter and 10 rows in stockinette, steam blocked it, and measured my stitch gauge. I'm not usually worried about row gauge since I make sure to steam and measure to my template rather than relying on the math.

Time to knit! I'll measure each section, make a few notes on my sketch, and set sail. After knitting for about an inch, I'll steam to the template, then recalculate if necessary for a different cast-on number or even a different needle size. Let's get started!

Read your knitting.

The way the stitches are seated on the needle is as important as the next direction in a pattern.

1 Make right front

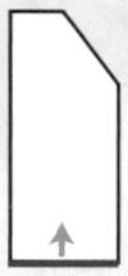

With C and smaller needle, cast on 32 (32, 32, 34, 34, 34). Knit 1 row, purl 1 row. Work Chart I, Chart II, Chart III, Chart II, Chart IV. Steam to template; note height of piece for V-neck.

Shape V-neck Change to larger needle and A. Working in Block Stitch, Dec 1 at beginning of every other RS row 10 (10, 10, 12, 14, 14) times, then every RS row 4 (4, 4, 2, 0, 0) times — 18 (18, 18, 20, 20, 20) stitches remain. Steam to template. Bind off.

Chart I

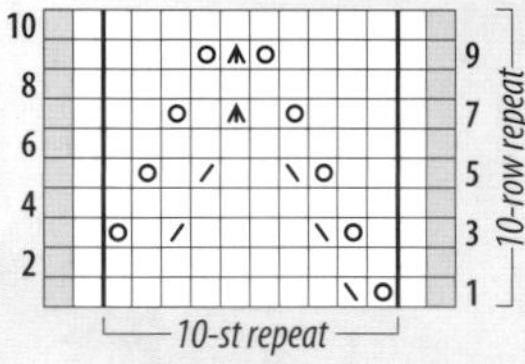

MULTIPLE OF 10 + 2 (4)

Row 1 (RS) K1 (2), **[yo, SSK, k8]** to last stitch(es), k1 (2).

Row 2 and all WS rows Purl.

Row 3 K1 (2), **[k1, yo, SSK, k4, k2tog, k1, yo]** to last stitch(es), k1 (2).

Row 5 K1 (2), **[k2, yo, SSK, k2, k2tog, k1, yo, k1]** to last stitch(es), k1 (2).

Row 7 K1 (2), **[k3, yo, k1, S2KP2, k1, yo, k2]** to last stitch(es), k1 (2).

Row 9 K1 (2), **[k4, yo, S2KP2, yo, k3]** to last stitch(es), k1 (2).

Work Rows 1–10 a total of 3 times.

Chart II

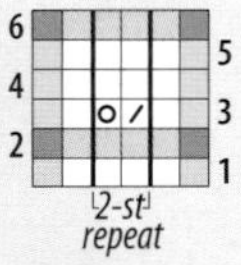

MULTIPLE OF 2

Rows 1, 2, 5, and 6 Knit.

Row 3 K1 (2), **[k2tog, yo]** to last stitch(es), k1 (2).

Row 4 Purl.

Chart III

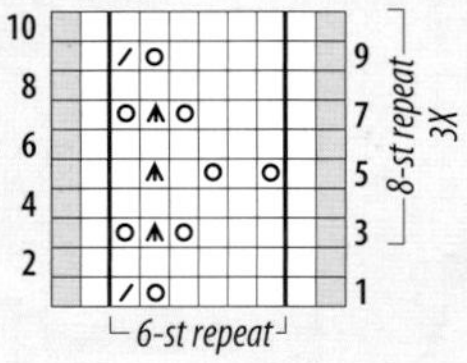

MULTIPLE OF 6 + 2 (4)

Row 1 (RS) K1 (2), **[k4, yo, k2tog]** to last stitch(es), k1 (2).

Row 2 and all WS rows Purl.

Row 3 K1 (2), **[k3, yo, S2KP2, yo]** to last stitch(es), k1 (2).

Row 5 K1 (2), **[yo, k1, yo, k1, S2KP2, k1]** to last stitch(es), k1 (2).

Row 7 K1 (2), **[k3, yo, S2KP2, yo]** to last stitch(es), k1 (2).

Row 9 K1 (2), **[k4, yo, k2tog]** to last stitch(es), k1 (2).

Work Rows 3–10 a total of 3 times.

Chart IV

MULTIPLE OF 10 + 2 (4)

Row 1 (RS) K1 (2), **[k4, yo, SSK, k4]** to last stitch(es), k1 (2).

Row 2 and all WS rows EXCEPT Row 22 Purl.

Row 3 K1 (2), **[k2, k2tog, yo, k1, yo, SSK, k3]** to last stitch(es), k1 (2).

Row 5 K1 (2), **[k1, k2tog, yo, k3, yo, SSK, k2]** to last stitch(es), k1 (2).

Row 7 K1 (2), **[k2tog, yo, k1, yo, S2KP2, yo, k1, yo, SSK, k1]** to last stitch(es), k1 (2).

Row 9 K1 (2), **[k2, yo, k1, S2KP2, k1, yo, k3]** to last stitch(es), k1 (2).

Row 11 K1 (2), **[k3, yo, S2KP2, yo, k4]** to last stitch(es), k1 (2).

Rows 13–20 Repeat Rows 1–8.

Rows 21 and 22 Knit.

DEC 1

At beginning of row SSK.

At end of row Work to last 2 stitches, k2tog.

BLOCK STITCH *MULTIPLE OF 6 + 1 (2)*

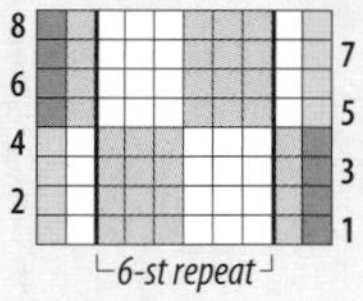

Rows 1–4 P1 (2), **[k3, p3]** to last stitch(es), k1 (2).

Rows 5–8 K1 (2), **[p3, k3]** to last stitch(es), p1 (2).

Repeat Rows 1–8.

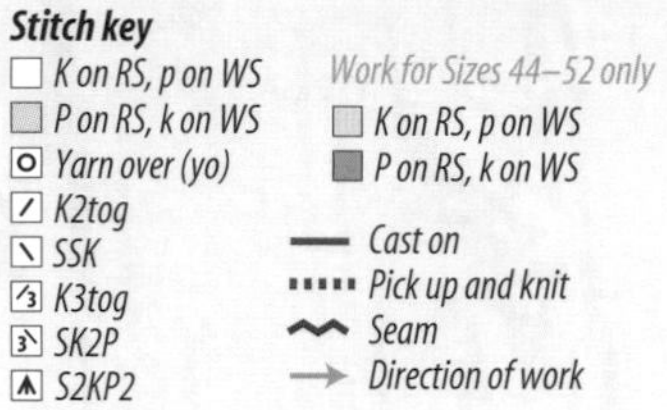

Stitch key

☐	K on RS, p on WS
▧	P on RS, k on WS
⊙	Yarn over (yo)
⟋	K2tog
⟍	SSK
⟋	K3tog
⟍	SK2P
▲	S2KP2

Work for Sizes 44–52 only

☐	K on RS, p on WS
▨	P on RS, k on WS

— Cast on
···· Pick up and knit
〜 Seam
→ Direction of work

2 Make strips for left front

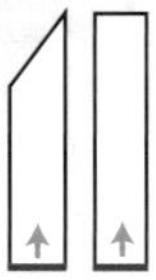

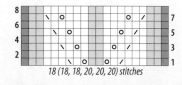

Center Strip With A and smaller needle, cast on 16 (16, 16, 18, 18, 18). **[Knit 1 row, purl 1 row]** twice, knit 4 rows. Repeat last 8 rows until piece is same height as right front to beginning of V-neck.

Shape V-neck Change to larger needle. Continuing in pattern, shape V-neck as for right front EXCEPT Dec 1 at end of RS rows — 2 stitches remain. SSK. Steam to template. Fasten off.

Shoulder Strip With D and smaller needle, cast on 18 (18, 18, 20, 20, 20). Work Chart V to shoulder. Steam to template. Bind off.

Chart V

WORKED OVER 18 (20) STITCHES

18 (18, 18, 20, 20, 20) stitches

Row 1 (RS) P2 (3), k3, k2tog, k1, yo, p2, yo, k1, SSK, k3, p2 (3).

Row 2 and all WS rows K2 (3), p6, k2, p6, k2 (3).

Row 3 P2 (3), k2, k2tog, k1, yo, k1, p2, k1, yo, k1, SSK, k2, p2 (3).

Row 5 P2 (3), k1, k2tog, k1, yo, k2, p2, k2, yo, k1, SSK, k1, p2 (3).

Row 7 P2 (3), k2tog, k1, yo, k3, p2, k3, yo, k1, SSK, p2 (3).

Repeat Rows 1–8.

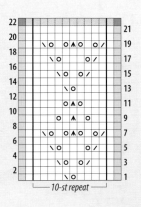

3 Add underarm panel to left front

Steam left front to template, placing marker at bottom of armhole at edge of shoulder strip. With RS facing, B, and smaller needle, pick up and knit (PUK) 3 stitches for every 4 rows between hem and marker. Knit 2 rows. **[Purl 1 row, knit 3 rows]** to underarm width. Steam to template. Bind off. Join strips for left front with Modified Mattress Stitch.

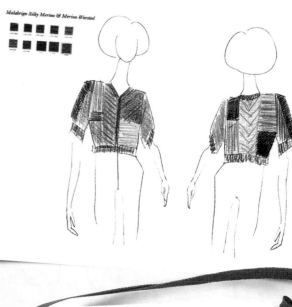

4 Make strips for back

Left strip

With D and smaller needle, cast on 18 (18, 18, 20, 20, 20). **Rows 1, 3, 5, 7 and 8** Knit. **Rows 2, 4, and 6** Purl. Work Rows 1–8 five more times. Change to A.

Row 1 **[K2, p2]** to last 2 stitches (end), k2 (0).
Rows 2, 4 Knit the purls and purl the knits.
Row 3 **[P2, k2]** to last 2 stitches (end), p2 (0).
Repeat last 4 rows to shoulder. Steam to template. Bind off.

Center strip

With B and larger needle, cast on 36 (36, 36, 36, 38, 38).
Work Chart VI to top of back neck of template. Steam to template. Bind off.

Chart VI

WORKED OVER 36 (38) STITCHES

Row 1 (RS) K1 (2), p3, k4, k3tog, yo, k1, yo, p3, k6, p3, yo, k1, yo, SK2P, k4, p3, k1 (2).
Row 2 and all WS rows Purl.
Row 3 K1 (2), p3, k2, k3tog, **[k1, yo]** twice, k1, p3, k6, p3, **[k1, yo]** twice, k1, SK2P, k2, p3, k1 (2).
Row 5 K1 (2), p3, k3tog, k2, yo, k1, yo, k2, p3, 3/3 LC, p3, k2, yo, k1, yo, k2, SK2P, p3, k1 (2).
Repeat Rows 1–6.

Stitch key
- ☐ K on RS, p on WS
- ▨ P on RS, k on WS
- ⊙ Yarn over (yo)
- ◿ K2tog
- ◺ SSK
- ◲ K3tog
- ◱ SK2P
- ⬦ 3/3 LC

3/3 LC Sl 3 to cn, hold to front, k3; k3 from cn.

Work for Sizes 48–52 only
- ☐ K on RS, p on WS
- ▨ P on RS, k on WS

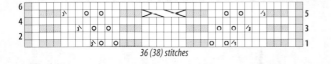

36 (38) stitches

Small: MALABRIGO Silky Merino in colors 27 Bobby Blue (A), 412 Teal Feather (B), 420 Light Hyacinth (C), and 418 London Sky (D)

a journey

Intermediate

Sizes

XS (S, M, L, 1X, 2X)
32 (36, 40, 44, 48, 52)"
Pick your size and make your life-size template (see page 126)

Light weight
650 (675, 750, 825, 875, 925) total yds as shown (40% each for A and B, 10% each for C and D)

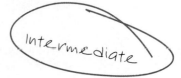

1"/2.5cm over stockinette stitch using smaller needle

4mm/US6, 4.5mm/US7, 60cm (24") or longer AND needle 1 or 2 sizes smaller for ribbing

Notes

See Techniques, page 120, for unfamiliar abbreviations and techniques.

Instructions are written for 6 sizes; when there is only 1 number, it applies to all sizes.

BOX STITCH *MULTIPLE OF 3 + 0 (2)*

Rows 1 and 3 (RS) K0 (1), **[p1, k2]** to end (last stitch), k0 (1).

Row 2 K0 (1), **[k1, p2]** to end (last stitch), k0 (1).

Row 4 Knit.

Repeat Rows 1–4.

Stitch key
☐ K on RS, p on WS
▨ P on RS, k on WS
☉ Yarn over (yo)
☑ K2tog
◺ SSK

Work for Sizes 48–52 only
▨ K on RS, p on WS

⊢ 9-st repeat ⊣

K2, P2 RIB *MULTIPLE OF 4 + 2*

RS rows [K2, p2] to last 2 stitches, k2.

WS rows [P2, k2] to last 2 stitches, p2.

Chart VII
MULTIPLE OF 9 + 0 (2)

Rows 1 and 5 (RS) K0 (1), **[k2, yo, SSK, k1, p4]** to end (last stitch), k0 (1).

Row 2 and all WS rows Purl.

Rows 3 and 7 K0 (1), **[k2tog, yo, k3, p4]** to end (last stitch), k0 (1).

Rows 9 and 13 K0 (1), **[p4, k3, yo, SSK]** to end (last stitch), k0 (1).

Rows 11 and 15 K0 (1), **[p4, k1, k2tog, yo, k2]** to end (last stitch), k0 (1).

Repeat Rows 1–16.

RIGHT STRIP

WORKED FROM THE SHOULDER DOWN

With C and smaller needle, cast on 18 (18, 18, 20, 20, 20). Work three 16-row repeats of Chart VII. Change to B and knit 2 rows. With A, work Box Stitch to bottom of template. Steam to template. Bind off.

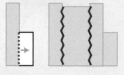

5 Add underarm panel to back

Work as for left front underarm panel EXCEPT PUK along right back strip. Join strips for back with Modified Mattress Stitch.

6 Knit sleeves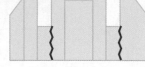

With A and smaller needle, work Basic Short Sleeve (page 116).

Cuff Change to ribbing needle and B. Purl 1 row. Work K2, P2 Rib for 2". Bind off in pattern.

7 Join strips and panels

Join left underarm panel to back and right underarm panel to front using Modified Mattress Stitch.

Optional: Work chain-stitch embroidery along seam between left front strips.

Steam to template. Sew shoulders and seam sleeves (page 118).

Hem With RS facing, B, and ribbing needle, PUK 1 stitch in every stitch along bottom edge, adjusting to a multiple of 4+2 on next row if necessary. Purl 1 row. Work 2" in K2, P2 Rib. Bind off in pattern.

Front band With RS facing, B, and ribbing needle, PUK 3 stitches in every 4 rows along right front edge, PUK 1 stitch in every stitch across back neck, then PUK 3 stitches for every 4 rows along left front edge, adjusting to a multiple of 4+2 on next row if necessary. Mark placement of 3 buttonholes along right front edge, with bottom buttonhole 1" from bottom of hem and next buttonholes 2½" apart. Purl 1 row. Work K2, P2 Rib for 4 rows, mark for buttonholes, work k2tog-yo for each buttonhole in next row. Continue in rib for 4 more rows. Bind off in pattern. Sew on buttons.

Alternate Route

Work chain-stitch embroidery at horizontal color changes on strips.

Great Plains

I designed this lightweight layer for those times of year when the seasons are changing. The large triangular panels are easy to knit and fit together for a figure-flattering effect. With two main colors, two different stitch patterns, and side panels and edge accents in a third color, this piece looks like it involves body shaping without any specific increases or decreases, other than those used in the triangles. The corrugated-rib front bands and striped sleeves add interest to the large expanses of solid color. Rather than using buttons, I chose linked closures as a fun contrast to the simple shapes.

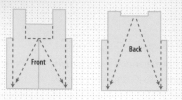

MASTER TEMPLATE

Front   Back

Extend style lines down from the outside shoulder for underarm panels. Divide fronts. Lower front neck 3" Draw diagonals from center neck to bottom of style lines.

CORRUGATED RIB
MULTIPLE OF 2 + 1
RS rows [K1C, p1A] to last stitch, k1C.
WS rows [P1C, k1A] to last stitch, p1C.

K2, P1 RIB
MULTIPLE OF 3 + 1
RS rows [K2, p1] to last 2 stitches, k2.
WS rows [P2, k1] to last 2 stitches, p2.

Alternate Route

Great Plains offers a wonderful opportunity for A-line shaping by including short rows in the side panels for a little more swing.

The sleeves can easily be extended to a long-sleeved version using the long-sleeve template.

This alternate sketch also shows a higher neckline. Start with a life-size template with your preferred neckline and draw the lines for the triangles from the neckline to the hem, allowing room for the button bands. Then measure those angles and knit away!

EASY +

Sizes

XS (S, M, L, IX, 2X)
32 (36, 40, 44, 48, 52)"

Pick your size and make your life-size template (see page 126).

10 ▦ 1"/2.5cm over
5 garter or seed stitch

4mm/US6 60cm (24") or longer AND needle 1 or 2 sizes smaller for sleeve trim

Medium weight 1025 (1075, 1175, 1275, 1375, 1425) total yards as shown (40% each for A and B; 20% for C)

Notes

See Techniques, p. 120, for unfamiliar abbreviations and techniques.

Increase rates are suggested for each angle, but angles will vary by a few degrees depending on the template size and any length adjustments you may make. See page 80 for measuring and knitting angles.

Small: PRISM YARNS Symphony in colors 106 (A), Violetta (B), and Bittersweet (C)

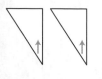

1 Make front triangles MAKE 2

25" in garter With B, cast on 1, kf&b — 2 stitches. **Next row** Kf&b, k1 — 3 stitches. Inc 1 on left edge only every 5 rows until triangle measures 15" from cast-on.

2 Make front sides MAKE 2

25" in seed With A, cast on 1, kf&b — 2 stitches. **Next row** Kf&b, k1 — 3 stitches. **[Inc 1 on left edge only every 4 rows, then every 5 rows]** until triangle measures 15" from cast-on. **Next row** Bind off 14 at increase edge. Work even on remaining stitches for 7". Bind off.

3 Make back triangle

35" in garter With B, cast on 1, kf&b&f — 3 stitches. Knit 2 rows. **Next row** Kf&b, k1, kf&b — 5 stitches. Inc 1 at beginning and end every 6 rows until triangle measures 22" from cast-on. Bind off.

4 Make back sides MAKE 2

With A, cast on 1, kf&b — 2 stitches. **Next row** Kf&b, k1 — 3 stitches. Inc 1 on right edge only every 7 rows until triangle measures 21" from cast-on. **Next row** Bind off 15 at increase edge. Work even on remaining stitches for 1". Bind off.

5 Join fronts and back

Sew together as shown using Modified Mattress Stitch. Steam pieces to template, marking bottom of armhole on each side back.

6 Add underarm panels

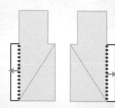

With C, pick up and knit between marker and hem; knit 1 row. **Rows 1–3** Knit. **Row 4** Purl. Repeat Rows 1–4 to fit template, then bind off on RS.

Sleeves

With B, work Basic Short Sleeve (page 116).
Cuff With smaller needle and A, work 6 rows in garter stitch. Change to C and knit 1 row, adjusting to a multiple of 3+2 if necessary. Work 1" in K2, P1 Rib. Bind off in pattern.

Finishing

Sew shoulders and seam sleeves (page 118). With C, work 2 rows single crochet along hem.

Neck trim

With C, work 2 rows single crochet around neck, placing decreases at each corner.

Bands

Left front With C and beginning at neck, PUK along front edge. **Next row** Knit. Work 7 rows Corrugated Rib, **Next row** (RS) Work 1 row K1, P1 Rib. **Next row** (WS) Knit. Bind off in pattern. **Right front** Repeat for second front, beginning at right front hem.
With C, work 1 round single crochet around entire body of garment, working increases at outer corners and decreases at inner corners. Attach toggles.

New DIRECTIONS

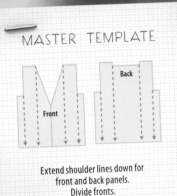

MASTER TEMPLATE

Front

Back

Extend shoulder lines down for
front and back panels.
Divide fronts.

I love a loooong color repeat! The way the self-striping yarns subtly change color has always intrigued me, because there are so many ways they can be used. My goal with this cardi was to highlight how the yarn looks completely different depending on the technique used—modular, bias, corrugated ribbing, and a textured stitch pattern.

One of the benefits of strip knitting, other than only having to knit across small areas at a time, is that the overall effect is very figure-flattering. The vertical lines create a lovely silhouette on any body type, and the bias knitting tends to create a narrower illusion—something many of us appreciate!

I've included a unique method of joining the strips with applied I-cord. It creates 3-D piping that accents those vertical lines.

Wisdom Poems

Kollage Temptation

or

Kollage Fantastic

Alternate Route

Try different stitch patterns. Test their gauge with a swatch: cast on the number suggested for the strip, knit a couple of inches, then steam to see if you need to adjust the cast-on count. Remember that cable, slip-stitch, or 2-color stranded patterns will decrease the width, so more stitches may be required. After a few inches, it's also safe to estimate how many rows will be needed to complete the strip. Count how many rows are in an inch, see how many inches you need, multiply, and you've got it. Try to pick a stitch pattern with a stitch or row multiple that will fit evenly into the strip.

Point of interest

Just one self-striping or long-repeat multi-color yarn offers many possibilities. Modular triangles and bias knitting change the direction of the stripes. Even when worked in the same direction and stitch, strips of different widths will vary. You can also control the color by starting at a different point in the sequence or by working from the center of one ball and the outside of another, as in New Direction's bias panels.

Size

XS (S, M, L, IX, 2X)

32 (36, 40, 44, 48, 52)".
Pick your size and make your life-size template (see page 126).

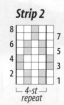

9 1"/2.5cm over garter stitch with A
4.5

6 1"/2.5cm over stockinette stitch with B
4

5mm/US8, 60cm (24") or longer

4 Medium weight

1400 (1450, 1575, 1750, 1875, 1925) total yards as shown (60% for A, 40% for B)

two 5mm/US8 double-pointed needles

six 19mm (3/4") buttons

Notes

See Techniques, page 120, for unfamiliar abbreviations and techniques.

Allow extra yardage if controlling color in a long-repeat multi-color yarn.

MOSS SLIPPED STITCH *MULTIPLE OF 2*

Slip all stitches purlwise with yarn at WS of work. Yarns alternate every other row.
Row 1 (WS) With A, k1, **[k1, sl 1]** to last stitch, k1.
Row 2 K1, **[sl 1, k1]** to last stitch, k1.
Row 3 With B, k1, **[sl 1, k1]** to last stitch, k1.
Row 4 K1, **[k1, sl 1]** to last stitch, k1.

DEC 1
At beginning of row SSK.
At end of row Work to last 2 stitches, k2tog.

INC 1
At beginning of row Kf&b in first stitch.
At end of row Kf&b in next to last stitch, k1.

Small: UNIVERSAL YARN/WISDOM YARNS Poems Silk in color 805 All the Way (A); SKACEL COLLECTION Simpliworsted by Hikoo in color 33 Red Hat Purple (B)

TEXTURE STITCH
MULTIPLE OF 4 + 1
Rows 1 and 5 K1, **[p1, k1]** to end.
Rows 2 and 6 P1, **[p1, k1]** to last stitch, p1.
Row 3 P1, **[k3, p1]** to end.
Row 4 **[K1, p3]** to last stitch, k1.
Row 7 K1, **[k1, p1, k2]** to end.
Row 8 **[P2, k1, p1]** to last stitch, p1.
Repeat Rows 1–8.

Strip 2

☐ Knit on RS, purl on WS
■ Purl on RS, knit on WS

JOINING STRIPS WITH APPLIED I-CORD

Make sure all pieces are steamed to schematic. Lining up adjacent strips with WS together, pin approximately every 2" from hem to shoulder.
Using double-pointed needles (dpn) and B, cast on 3 stitches, then insert the left tip of the same needle through 1 edge stitch of each piece starting at the hem.
Slide all stitches to right tip of same needle, k2, SK2P (last cast-on stitch and 2 picked-up stitches), PUK2 more stitches (1 from each edge). Repeat from until 3 stitches remain on needle at shoulder edge, SK2P, cut yarn, and fasten off.

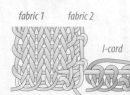

fabric 1   fabric 2

I-cord

Cast on 3, slide 2 edge stitches onto left tip of needle, slide to right tip.

K2, sl 1, k2 edge stitches together,…

…psso to complete.

Shown laid flat, 3 rows joined.

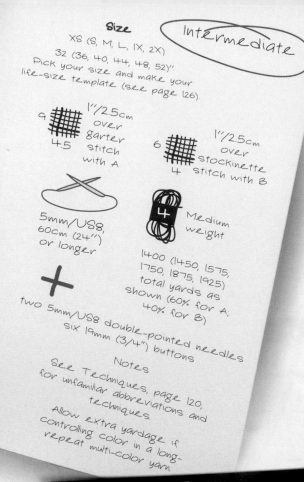

40

1 Make left diagonal strip and right diagonal strip

Work in garter stitch with A. For striped effect used on front strips, use 2 balls of A, working 2 rows from center of 1 ball and 2 rows from outside of other ball. Change yarns at beginning of every RS row.

Left strip Cast on 1, kf&b&f—3 stitches. **Next row** Inc 1, knit to end. Inc 1 at beginning of every row AND change yarn at beginning of every RS row until bottom edge measures 3½ (3½, 3½, 3½, 3¾, 3¾)" wide (approximately 23 (23, 23, 23, 25, 25) stitches). Steam to template.

Work even in diagonal garter stripes: Inc 1 at beginning and Dec 1 at end of every RS row until left edge measures 11" from cast-on. Continue to Inc 1 at beginning and Dec 1 at end of every RS row AND AT SAME TIME, shape V-neck as follows: Dec 1 at beginning of every other WS row 17 (17, 17, 20, 19, 19) times, then every WS row 3 (3, 3, 0, 3, 3) times—3 stitches remain. Sl 1, k2tog, psso. Steam to template. Cut yarn and fasten off.

Right strip Work as for left diagonal strip EXCEPT reverse diagonal by Dec 1 at beginning and Inc 1 at end of RS rows AND Dec 1 at end of WS rows for neck shaping.

2 Make 4 shoulder strips
2 for front and 2 for back

With A, cast on 17 (17, 17, 25, 25, 25). Work in Texture Stitch to shoulder. Steam to template. Bind off.

3 Join a shoulder strip to each diagonal strip

Join diagonal strips to shoulder strips with applied I-cord.

4 Make back panel

a
Work first triangle of center panel

With A, cast on 1, kf&b&f—3 stitches. Working in garter stitch, Inc 1 at beginning of every row until triangle measures 7 (7, 7, 7, 7½, 7½)" wide, end with an odd number of stitches—approximately 45 (45, 45, 45, 47, 47) stitches. Do not bind off. Cut yarn.

b
Add second triangle

Row 1 (RS) Join new yarn, kl&b into first stitch, place marker, k2tog to join with first triangle, turn—3 stitches. **Row 2 and all WS rows** Knit. **Row 3** Kf&b, k1, slip marker (sm), k2tog, turn—4 stitches. **Row 5** Kf&b, knit to marker, sm, k2tog. Repeat Rows 5 and 6 until all stitches from first triangle have been joined, end with a WS row. Do not bind off. Cut yarn.

c
Change color and work third triangle

Row 1 (RS) Join new yarn and knit to last 2 stitches, k2tog. **Row 2 and all WS rows** Sl 1, knit to end. **Row 3** Knit to last 2 stitches, k2tog. Repeat Rows 3 and 4 until 3 stitches remain, end with a WS row. SK2P, cut yarn, and fasten off.

d
Add last triangle

Pick up and knit (PUK) 1 stitch between each garter ridge along top edge of third triangle. **Next row** (WS) Knit. **Row 1** SSK, knit to last 2 stitches, k2tog. **Row 2** Sl 1, knit to end. Repeat Rows 1 and 2 until 3 stitches remain, end with a WS row. SK2P, cut yarn, and fasten off. Steam to template.

5 Join a shoulder strip to each side of back panel

Mark 1" down from each shoulder strip. Join shoulder strip to back panel between bottom and marker with applied I-cord.

6 Add underarm panels to fronts and back

Block fronts and back to template, placing markers at bottom of armhole at outer edge of each shoulder strip. With RS facing and B, PUK 1 stitch for every 2 rows between marker and bottom. Knit 2 rows. **[Purl 1 row, knit 3 rows]** to underarm width. Steam to template. Bind off.

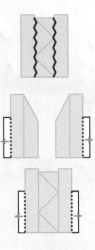

— Cast on
····· Pick up and knit
〜 Seam
⁝⁝⁝⁝ Stitches on hold
→ Direction of work

Knit sleeves

With B, work Basic Long Sleeve (page 116), EXCEPT at 4" less than desired length, end with a RS row. **[Purl 1 row, knit 3 rows]** 4 times.

Cuff Join A and work five 4-row repeats of Moss Slipped Stitch. Cut A. With B, knit 2 rows. Bind off.

Finishing

Sew shoulders and seam sleeves (page 118).

With RS facing and B, pick up stitches evenly around hem (see Pick-up rates, page 118) and knit 2 rows; do not cut yarn. Join A and work as for cuff.

Mark right front for 6 buttonholes with the first ½" from the beginning of neck shaping and the last 1" from the bottom. With RS facing, B, and beginning at lower edge of right front, pick up and knit around front and neck edges at the following rates: 4 stitches for every 3 garter ridges along vertical and diagonal edges and 1 stitch for every ridge across back neck. Knit 1 row, placing markers at both back I-cords. Knit 12 more rows, AND on every RS row k2tog at I-cord markers, AND on 5th row work yo-k2tog at each buttonhole marker. Bind off.

"Creativity
is
just a
process."

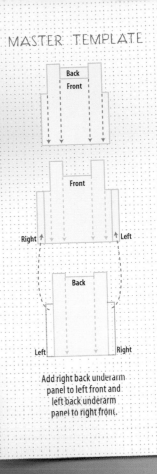

Add right back underarm panel to left front and left back underarm panel to right front.

Crossroads

A pullover's wider center-front panel offers possibilities for design that focus the eye front and center. Stacked chevrons create an interesting pattern that lends itself to the rectangular shape. I chose a hand-dyed self-striping yarn with a very long color repeat, and started by dividing the ball into smaller balls at the color breaks. I added 3 coordinating semisolids for the back panels and to supplement the smaller balls for the mitered front.

Because there was such a strong design on the front panel, and since the sleeves continue the gradient effect, I chose plain color blocked panels for the sides and back. Garter ridges create vertical piping between the panels and accent the neckline and hem.

Alternate Route

The center front panel can easily be adapted for a sweetheart neckline by modifying the second chevron section. Cast on the full number of stitches (49 in this case) and mark the center (25th) stitch, then continue as for the first section. If you prefer the focal point higher, knit the first chevron for as many additional rows as you'd like — just remember to subtract the same number of rows from the second chevron so the panel length stays the same.

The overall silhouette can also be changed to more of an A-line shape by simply adding short rows in the side panels as described on page 127.

EASY +

Size
XS (S, M, L, IX, 2X)
32 (36, 40, 44, 48, 52)"

Pick your size and make your
life-size template (see page 126).

Light weight

10 ⊞ 1''/2.5cm
over
garter
5   stitch

1325 (1375, 1500, 1650,
1775, 1850) total yards
(allow extra yardage
for A if controlling
color in a long-
repeat multi-color)

4mm/US6,
60cm (24'')
or longer

removable
stitch markers
crochet hook

Notes
See Techniques, page 120, for
unfamiliar abbreviations and techniques.

BROKEN RIB *MULTIPLE OF 2 + 1*
Row 1 (RS) Knit.
Row 2 **[K1, p1]** to last stitch, k1.
Repeat Rows 1 and 2.

DEC 1
At beginning of RS rows K1, SSK.
At end of RS rows K2tog, k1.

Point of interest
Here, the focus of the center panel is mid-
panel, but you can shift it up or down by simply
working more ridges in one mitered section
and fewer in the other.

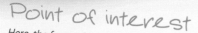

Small: FREIA FINE HANDPAINT YARNS
Ombre Sport in color Vertigo (A);
Semi-Solid Sport in colors Viridian (B),
and Swamp (C)

CONTROL THE COLORS

Divide 1 ball of A into separate colors
(Vertigo separated into 4 balls). For
striped chevron sections, change color
at beginning of RS rows as desired.

1 Make front panel

Knit 2 chevron sections

With A, cast on 1. **Row 1** (RS) Knit in front and back and front (Kf&b&f) of cast-on stitch — 3 stitches. **Row 2** Knit. **Row 3** Kf&b, kf&b, k1 — 5 stitches. Mark center stitch with removable marker. **Row 4** Knit. **Row 5** Kf&b, knit to 1 stitch before marked stitch, kf&b, kf&b in marked stitch, knit to last 2 stitches, kf&b, k1 — 4 stitches increased. **Row 6 and all WS rows** Knit. Work Rows 5 and 6 a total of 11 times (12 garter ridges) — 49 stitches.

All remaining RS rows K1, SSK, knit to marked stitch, kf&b&f in marked stitch, knit to last 3 stitches, k2tog, k1 — 49 stitches. Work until piece measures 6½" along each side and approximately 9" in the center, end with a WS row.

FOR SIZE L ONLY Work 2 more rows.

FOR SIZES 1X–2X ONLY Work 4 more rows.

Place stitches before marked stitch on one holder; place remaining stitches on another holder. Make second mitered section.

Join with 2 side triangles

With WS of chevron sections facing and A, knit across first holder from one section and second holder from other section — 49 stitches. **Row 1** K1, k2tog, knit to 1 stitch before marked stitch, SK2P, knit to last 3, SSK, k1 — 4 stitches decreased. **Row 2 and all WS rows** Knit. Repeat Rows 1 and 2 until 5 stitches remain. **Next RS row** K1, SK2P, k1 — 3 stitches. **Next row** SK2P, cut yarn, and fasten off. Repeat for other side triangle.

Add edging to center panel

With RS facing and B, pick up and knit (PUK) 5 stitches for every 4 ridges along right edge of center panel. Knit 3 (3, 3, 3, 5, 5) rows. Bind off. Repeat on left edge of panel. Steam to template.

2 Make 4 shoulder strips

2 in A for front and 2 in C for back

Cast on 23 (23, 23, 25, 25, 25). Work in Broken Rib to shoulder. End with a WS row. Steam to template. Bind off.

3 Join shoulder strips to front panel

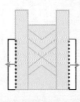

Mark 4" down from top of each front shoulder strip, align with top of center panel, and join right shoulder strip to right edging and left shoulder strip to left edging with Modified Mattress Stitch.

4 Add underarm panels

Steam front to template, placing marker at bottom of armhole at outer edge of each shoulder strip. With RS facing and B, PUK 2 stitches for every 3 rows along left edge between marker and hem. Work in garter stitch to underarm width. End with a WS row. Steam to template. Bind off. Repeat along right edge, EXCEPT PUK between hem and marker.

5 Make back

Add center panel to left back shoulder strip

Mark 1" down from top of each back shoulder strip. With RS of one strip facing and B, PUK 2 stitches for every 3 rows along right edge between hem and marker. Work in garter stitch to width of back neck, end with a WS row. Steam to template. Bind off.

Join right shoulder strip to center panel

Sew other back shoulder strip to center panel from marker to hem with Modified Mattress Stitch.

Sleeves

With A, cast on 80 (80, 90, 96,100, 100). Work even in stockinette for 6 (16, 26, 32, 40, 50) rows. Mark each end of row for underarm. Dec 1 each side of next RS row, then every 6 rows 14 (12, 10, 13, 8, 6) times, then every 4 rows 0 (0, 5, 4, 9, 11) times — 50 (54, 58, 60, 64, 64) stitches. Work even to 13½ (13½, 14, 15, 15, 15)". With B, knit 7 rows. Bind off.

Finishing

Sew underarm panels to left and right back shoulder strips. Sew shoulders and seam sleeves (page 118).

With B, half double crochet evenly around neckline, decreasing in each corner.

With RS facing and B, PUK around hem at the following rates: 1 stitch between each garter ridge and 2 stitches for every 3 stitches across Broken Rib panel. Place marker and join to work in the round. **[Knit 1 round, purl 1 round]** 3 times. Bind off.

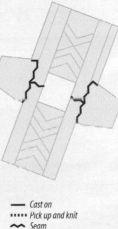

——— Cast on
······· Pick up and knit
〰〰 Seam
⁞⁞⁞ Stitches on hold
→ Direction of work

Magical Milestones

These tops combine a few of my favorite things: tee shaping, modular piecing, bias knitting, and quilt-block layouts. I love all fiber arts and see many possibilities that translate to knitting. I'll often see fabric or a quilt and think, "I could knit that!" Since we can knit squares and rectangles to any size we like, it's easy to translate quilt block patterns into knit designs. Here the half-square triangle quilt block is worked with bias-knit squares.

The real fun comes in deciding on the block layout. Magical Milestones has a center panel of 12 two-color squares—6 high and 2 wide. Star Traveler is 24 similar squares arranged 6 high and 4 wide—half the blocks are in one color combination and the other half are in another, yet one color is common to all 24 blocks.

Arranging the blocks provides endless opportunities for entertainment and experimentation—limited only by your creativity. Play with the blocks until you find an arrangement you like, then seam them together.

Instructions for Magical Milestones begin on page 50 and for Star Traveler on page 52.

Star traveler

I developed a map for the layout. As I knit, I joined the squares a few at a time into horizontal strips — fewer pieces to keep track of and an increasing sense of momentum.

Quilt-block layouts

This 2×6 grid can be filled with half-square triangles in various combinations. We chose a 2-color combo. Make each square, then arrange and assemble them into a center panel. Choose your favorite layout and enjoy.

A grid of four squares across and 6 high offers even more possibilities for the half-square-triangle block arrangements. Photocopy or scan one of the layouts, or choose a blank and create your own.

Start with your choice of three colors and use colored pencils (or the fill option in a paint program) to try different combinations. The easiest part of this knitting is that you start with one cast-on stitch and increase to the diagonal width of the square, then change color and decrease back to 1 and bind off. Once you know how wide that is, the rest of the squares will be made the same way using the color combination of your choice.

Once your layout is planned, you are free to knit away.

All these designs are made using 12 half-square triangle blocks.

knit in new directions →→→

This sweater is full of bias knitting.

I'm a fan of bias knitting for its overall slimming effect, so Magical Milestones is completed with bias side panels. No waist shaping is used, but the effect creates a sleek silhouette. The back panel is a mitered chevron but can easily be replaced with another set of blocks — it's totally up to you!

Color blocking on the sides and back really sets off the front patterning of Star Traveler, but feel free to continue blocks on the back if you prefer — the same layout as the front or something entirely different. The vertical garter ridges on either side of the front and back panels can be widened as much as you'd like for an even more oversized fit. The longer back panel allows for a comfortable fit, especially when sitting!

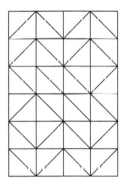
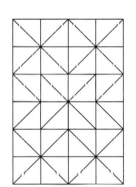
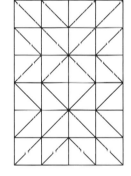
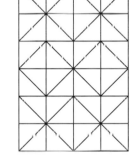
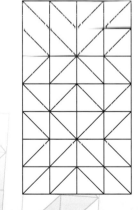
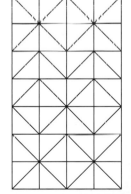

See Techniques, page 120, for unfamiliar abbreviations and techniques.

EASY +

Sizes
S/M (M/L, 1X/2X)
39 (46, 56)"

1"/2.5cm over garter stitch

5.5

3.75mm/US5, 60cm (24") or longer

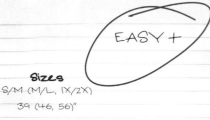

3

Light weight

1025 (1200, 1350) total yards as shown (65% for A; 25% for B; and 10% for C)

INC 1
At beginning of row Kf&b in first stitch.
At end of row Kf&b in next to last stitch, k1.

1 Make squares
Increase triangle
With A, cast on 1, kf&b&f—3 stitches.
Rows 1–23 Inc 1, knit to end—26 stitches at end of Row 23. Cut yarn.

Add decrease triangle
Row 24 Change to C and knit.
Rows 25–47 Knit to last 2 stitches, k2tog—3 stitches at end of Row 47.
Row 48 SK2P. Cut yarn and fasten off. Steam to 3½" square.

Make 11 more

2 Arrange squares
Position to create a pattern. Whipstitch squares together to form two vertical strips, stitching through purl bumps at edge of each row.

3 Sew strips together
Whipstitch strips together for front panel. Steam to 7" × 21".

21"

7"

4 Add trim
With RS facing and B, pick up and knit (PUK) 4 stitches for every 3 ridges along long side of panel—approximately 96 stitches. Knit 7 (7, 9) rows. Cut yarn. Join A and knit 4 (6, 8) rows. Bind off. Repeat along other side.

9½ (10, 11)"

5 Make back panel
Increase section
With C, cast on 3.
Row 1 [Kf&b] twice, k1—5 stitches. Mark center stitch with removable marker and move it up as you knit.
Row 2 and all WS rows Knit.
Row 3 and all RS rows until bottom edge measures 7" Kf&b, knit to 1 before marked stitch, kf&b, kf&b in marked stitch, knit to last 2 stitches, kf&b, k1 — 4 stitches increased—approximately 49 stitches after last increase row.

Straight section
RS rows Dec 1, knit to 1 before marked stitch, kf&b, kf&b in marked stitch, knit to last 2 stitches, Dec 1.
WS rows Knit. Continue until the center length of the panel measures 21", steamed.

Decrease section
Next RS row Dec 1, knit to 2 stitches before center, k3tog, place remaining stitches on hold. Work each triangle separately as follows: *First half* Dec 1 at beginning and end of every RS row until 2 stitches remain. *Next RS row* SSK. Cut yarn and fasten off. *Second half* Return remaining stitches to needle, ready to work a RS row. Work as for first half.

6 Add trim
Work Step 4 as for front panel.

directions → → →

DEC 1
At beginning of row SSK.
At end of row Work to last 2 stitches, k2tog.

GARTER RIDGE
[Knit 1 row, purl 1 row] 3 times, knit 2 rows. Repeat last 8 rows.

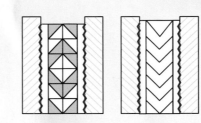

Alternate Route
Rearrange the blocks to create desired design. Instead of a mitered panel, create blocks for the back as well.

7 Make side panels
Left side
Work lower corner...
With B, cast on 1, kf&b&f—3 stitches. Work in Garter Ridge pattern and AT SAME TIME, Inc 1 at beginning and end on 3 of every 4 rows until bottom edge measures 5 (6½, 8½)".

...left bias section...
Continue in pattern and AT SAME TIME, Inc 1 at beginning and Dec 1 at end of every RS row until long side measures 22½".

...and upper corner
Dec 1 at beginning and end on 3 of every 4 rows until 3 stitches remain. SK2P. Cut yarn and fasten off.

Right side
Work lower corner...

...right bias section...
Continue in pattern and AT SAME TIME, Dec 1 at beginning and Inc 1 at end of RS rows until long side measures 22½".

...and upper corner

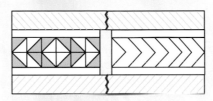

□ A
□ C
— Cast on
••••• Pick up and knit
～ Seam
⊔⊔⊔⊔ Stitches on hold
→ Direction of work

8 Assemble panels
Sew side panels to front and back panels
Position center front panel between a right- and left-side panel as shown, matching bottom edges and leaving 1½" to shoulder. Use mattress stitch to join.
Repeat for center back panel EXCEPT leave ½" to shoulder.

Sew shoulders
Sew front to back at shoulders.

9 Add sleeve bands
Measure 8½ (9½, 10)" from shoulder seam along front and back for armholes and place markers. With B, PUK102 (114, 120) stitches between markers.
Purl 1 row. Work 0 (0, 4) rows stockinette, two 8-row repeats of Garter Ridge pattern, then 8 rows of stockinette. Cut yarn. Join A and knit 4 rows. Bind off.

Finishing
Sew side and underarm seams.
Neckline trim With A, work 1 round of single crochet, slip stitch to join, then work 1 round of reverse single crochet.
Hem trim With A, PUK along hem edge; do not join. Knit 5 rows. Bind off. Sew ends together.

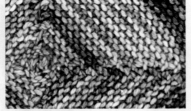

Interlocking edges

S/M: MALABRIGO Arroyo in colors 49 Jupiter (A), 48 Glitter (B), and 866 Arco Iris (C)

a journey into creativity →→→   51

Small: BERROCO Ultra Alpaca Light in colors 4294 Turquoise Mix (A), 4275 Pea Soup Mix (B), 4285 Oceanic Mix (C), and 4277 Peat Mix (D)

INC 1
At beginning of row Kf&b in first stitch.
At end of row Kf&b in next to last stitch, k1.

DEC 1
At beginning of row SSK.
At end of row Work to last 2 stitches, k2tog.

1 Make squares

Increase triangle
Cast on 1, kf&b&f — 3 stitches.
Rows 1–20 Kf&b, knit to end — 23 stitches at end of Row 20.

Add decrease triangle
Row 21 (RS) Change color and knit to last 2 stitches, k2tog.
Rows 22–40 Knit to last 2 stitches, k2tog — 3 stitches at end of Row 40.
Row 41 SK2P. Cut yarn and fasten off.

2 Make 12 (12, 14) in A/B...

...and 12 (12, 14) in A/C

2 Arrange in rows
Whipstitch squares together to form 6 (6, 7) rows, stitching through purl bumps at edge of each square. Steam each row to 3" × 12".

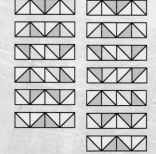

3 Sew rows together
Whipstitch 6 (6, 7) rows together for front panel.

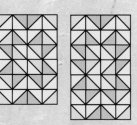

Sizes
XS/S (M/L, 1X/2X)
39 (49, 59)"

EASY +

10 [grid] 1"/2.5cm over 5 garter

3

Light weight 900 (1050, 1175) total yards as shown (50% for A; 30% for D; 10% each for B and C)

3.75mm/US5
60cm (24") or longer

Notes
See Techniques, page 120, for unfamiliar abbreviations and techniques.

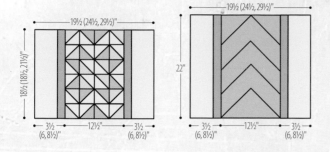

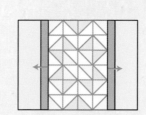

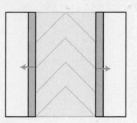

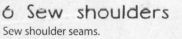

4 Make back panel

Increase section

With A, cast on 1, kf&b&f—3 stitches.
Row 1 (RS) Kf&b, kf&b&f, kf&b — 7 stitches.
Row 2 and all WS rows Knit. Mark center stitch with removable marker and move it up as you knit.
Row 3 and all RS rows until bottom edge measures 12½" Kf&b, knit to 1 before marked stitch, kf&b, kf&b in marked stitch, knit to last 2 stitches, kf&b, k1 — 4 stitches increased

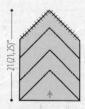

Straight section

RS rows Dec 1, knit to 1 before marked stitch, kf&b, kf&b in marked stitch, knit to last 2 stitches, Dec 1.
WS rows Knit.
Continue until the center length of the panel measures 21 (21, 25)", steamed.

Decrease section

Next RS row Dec 1, knit to 2 stitches before center, k3tog, place remaining stitches on hold. Work each triangle separately as follows: *First half* Dec 1 at beginning and end of every RS row until 2 stitches remain.
Next RS row SSK. Cut yarn and fasten off.
Second half Return remaining stitches to needle, ready to work a RS row. Work as for first half. Steam to 12½" × 21 (21, 25)".

〰 *Seam*
ⅲⅲⅲ *Live stitches*
→ *Direction of work*

5 Add side panels

With RS facing and D, pick up and knit (PUK)17 along each block at left edge of center front panel — 102 (102, 119) stitches. Knit 13 (19, 21) rows. Change to A and knit 2 rows, adjusting to 104 (104, 120) on last row. Work 1 (2, 3) sixteen-row repeats of Flame Stitch (instructions on page 101), end with a WS row. Bind off 68 (68, 76), place remaining 36 (36, 44) stitches on hold for sleeve. Repeat along right edge of panel. With RS facing and D, PUK116 (116, 132) along left edge of center back panel. Continue as for front side panels EXCEPT adjust to 120 (120, 136) on second row of A AND bind off 80 (80, 88)

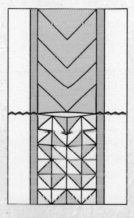

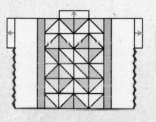

6 Sew shoulders

Sew shoulder seams.

7 Add bands

Neckband

With RS facing and C, PUK16 stitches for every square across front neck edge and 64 across back, place a removable marker on stitch at each shoulder, and join to work in the round. Purl 1 round. **[(Knit to 1 stitch before marker, S2KP2) twice; purl 1 round]** 5 times. Bind off loosely.

Sleeve band

With RS facing and A, place stitches from hold onto needle. Knit 12 rows. Bind off.

Finishing

Sew side seams from underarm to 4" above end of front. Sew sleeve seams.

Use tank shaping. Extend
inside shoulder lines down
for front and back panels.

Audacious angles

Now let's explore another option within panels — triangles with textured stitch patterns.

For this tank, my swatch was a 60-degree triangle in garter stitch. It was easy and hands-on: I followed the rate of increase suggested in the chart on page 80. After an inch, I checked how closely the knitting matched the desired angle. Since it steamed right into place, I continued at that rate until the triangle was 7½" tall — the measurement I needed for the panel width. The length of each side was 8½", so arranging 3 triangles made a panel 17" long. Adding half a triangle to each end, squared off the rectangle. These halves are knit as 30-degree triangles.

I knew I wanted to make triangles in different stitch patterns and that this might require adjusting the rate of increase. Since the triangles are knit separately, it's easy: just steam to the template, and adjust the rate if necessary. I do give suggested rates, but that is all they are — suggestions. What is important is to create the correct angle and to make the triangle the size you need. Exact row count is not as important, since the triangle is measured to the template and bound off when it fits.

I used a bright accent color for ridges between the triangles and as side panels — for a slimming silhouette, keep this a darker color. Curving the armholes gives a nice fit for a sleeveless top.

In the sketch: *Stockinette long sleeves*

Alternate Route

Adding short rows to the side panels will create an A-line top. Check out page 127 to see how easily this can be done.

Also, by using the original template for the pullover, a long-sleeved version can be made. Add garter ribs at the wrist for a nice design detail.

Another option would be to knit an entire back panel in one pattern stitch — like garter, moss, or waffle stitch — in the same color as the sleeves.

INC 1

At beginning (end) of row
Kf&b in first (last) stitch.

DEC 1

At end of RS (WS) rows Work to
last 2 stitches, k2tog (SSP).
At beginning of RS (WS) rows
SSK (p2tog).

HDC

With C, work half double crochet.

SEEDED WAFFLE

MULTIPLE OF 2
Row 1 (RS) [**K1, p1**] to end.
Row 2 Knit the purls and
purl the knits.
Rows 3 and 4 Knit.
Repeat Rows 1–4.

☐ *Knit on RS, purl on WS*
☐ *Purl on RS, knit on WS*

ANDALUSIAN STITCH *MULTIPLE OF 2*

Rows 1 and 3 (RS) Knit.
Row 2 Purl.
Row 4 [**K1, p1**] to end.
Repeat Rows 1–4.

BOX STITCH

MULTIPLE OF 3
Rows 1 and 3 (RS) Knit.
Row 2 Purl.
Row 4 [**K2, p1**] to end.
Repeat Rows 1–4.

SEED STITCH *MULTIPLE OF 2*

Row 1 (RS) [**K1, p1**] to end.
All remaining rows Knit the purl
stitches and purl the knit stitches.

How to Knit the TRIANGLES

Steam triangles to templates.

The angles

Triangle 1, 60° Equilateral

With A, cast on 1, kf&b&f—3 stitches.
Rows 1, 2, and 4 Knit.
Row 3 Kf&b, knit to last stitch,
kf&b—2 stitches increased.
Continue to increase at beginning
and end every 4 rows until 7½"
from tip to center stitch on needle;
note the number of stitches and
garter ridges.

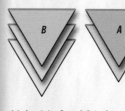

Make 2 in Seed Stitch and A.
Make 2 in Seeded Waffle and B.
Make 1 in Andalusian Stitch and B.
Make 2 in garter stitch and D.
Hdc along bound-off edge.

Triangle 2, 30° Left

With A, cast on 1, kf&b —
2 stitches.
Rows 1, 2, and 4 Knit.
Row 3 Knit to last stitch,
kf&b —1 stitch increased.
*Mark increase edge, and
increase on that edge only:*
Continue to increase every
4 rows until the same
number of garter ridges
have been worked as in
Triangle 1. Bind off.

Make 1 in garter stitch
and B. Hdc along
diagonal edge.

Triangle 3, 30° Right

With A, cast on 1, kf&b —
2 stitches.
Rows 1, 2, and 4 Knit.
Row 3 Kf&b, knit to end —
1 stitch increased.
*Mark increase edge, and
increase on that edge only:*
Continue to increase every 4
rows until the same number of
garter ridges have been worked
as in Triangle 1. Bind off.

Make 1 in garter stitch and A.
Make 1 in garter stitch and D.
Make 1 in Seed Stitch and A.
Hdc along diagonal edge
of garter D triangle.

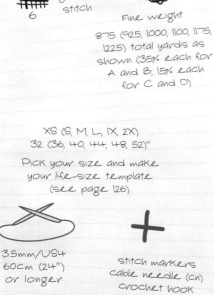

Intermediate

2.5cm/1"
12 ☐ over
garter
6 stitch

Fine weight

875 (925, 1000, 1100, 1175,
1225) total yards as
shown (35% each for
A and B; 15% each
for C and D)

XS (S, M, L, 1X, 2X)
32 (36, 40, 44, 48, 52)"

Pick your size and make
your life-size template
(see page 126).

3.5mm/US4
60cm (24")
or longer

stitch markers
cable needle (cn)
crochet hook

See Techniques, page 120, for
unfamiliar abbreviations and techniques.

See Making the Shapes on page 80.

Assemble the panels

Make the triangles, working in stitch patterns and colors as indicated. Arrange all triangles with hdc edges as shown on panel templates. Modified Mattress Stitch triangle edges to hdc edges.

Steam to schematic measurements.

FRONT & BACK, SIZES 48–52 ONLY With C, hdc 2 rows across top and bottom edges of panels.

FRONT & BACK, SIZE 44 ONLY With C, hdc 1 row across top and bottom edges of panels.

1 Add left panel to front panel

With RS facing and C, and beginning at the bottom of Front Panel, pick up and knit (PUK) 108 (108, 108, 111, 114, 114) along edge.

SIZES 48–52 ONLY Knit 4 rows.

ALL SIZES Cast on 24 — 132 (132, 132, 135, 138, 138) stitches.

Begin Box Stitch Work Row 4, then work Rows 1–4 to shoulder width of template, end with a RS row.

Shape armhole on next WS row Bind off 32 (32, 38, 42, 45, 45) and continue in pattern to end of row.

Dec 1 at end of every RS row AND at beginning of every WS row on next 16 rows — 84 (84, 78, 78, 78, 78) stitches. Cut yarn. With D, work garter stitch to width of template.

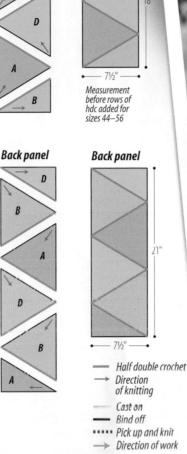

Front panel

Front panel

18"

7½"

Measurement before rows of hdc added for sizes 44–56

Back panel

Back panel

21"

7½"

── Half double crochet
→ Direction of knitting
── Cast on
── Bind off
•••• Pick up and knit
→ Direction of work

2 Add right panel to front panel

SIZES 32–44 ONLY With C, cast on 24, then, with RS facing and beginning at top of Front Panel, PUK108 (108, 111, 114) along edge — 132 (132, 135, 138) stitches.

SIZES 48–52 ONLY With C and beginning at top of Front Panel, PUK114 along edge. Knit 3 rows. Cast on 24 — 138 stitches.

ALL SIZES Continue as for Left Panel EXCEPT bind off for armhole on a RS row AND Dec 1 at beginning of RS and end of WS rows.

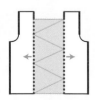

3 Add right and left side panels to back panel

Right panel Work as for Left Front EXCEPT PUK126 (126, 126, 129, 132, 132) along edge of Back Panel and cast on 6.

Left panel Work as for Right Front EXCEPT cast on 6 and PUK126 (126, 126, 129, 132, 132) along left edge of Back Panel.

Perfect for warm weather, this sleeveless version incorporates a curved armhole for a sleek fit.

Shown in Small: CLAUDIA HAND PAINTED YARNS Fingering in colors Blue Terra Cotta (A), Honey (B), Paprika (C), and Lakeside Liz (D)

Finishing

Sew shoulder and side seams. With C, sc around armhole edges. With C, hdc around neckline and hem.

When single crocheting around an open edge, decrease in the corners for a clean, sharp finish.

2-to-1 decrease: Work a stitch to its last step, work the next stitch to its last step, then pull yarn through all loops on hook (shown above in single crochet).

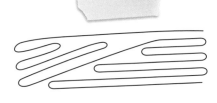

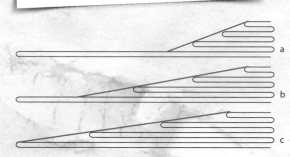

When the first short-row pair of a wedge is the longest, it establishes the slant of the following pairs.

CREATIVE SHORT ROWS

The same short rows that shape knits at shoulders and heels can be purely decorative. They can create interesting shapes that imitate intarsia. They can change the slant of the rows; when combined with changes in color or texture, this can be a strong design element.

A wedge is a short-row section. **Short rows** are partial rows of knitting that stop short of the opposite edge and then return to form a second partial (short) row. Because we work across and back, we label them as **short-row pairs** — work a row in one direction, stopping short of the edge, then work back with a second row. We say **work** because short rows can be worked in many combinations of knit and purl, including garter, stockinette, and seed stitch.

Think of the rows as the grain of our fabric. When we change the slant by working rows that don't extend all the way across (short rows), we change the grain. When you work the full row at the end of one wedge, you establish the slant for the next wedge.

For creative short rows, I start each wedge with the longest pair of short rows, with each following pair progressively shorter. You could start with the shortest pair and make each pair progressively longer, but I don't use this method.

I often work garter ridges (a pair or two of knit rows) across the fabric between wedges for added interest. They bend and flow as they follow the short-row shaping — this is truly creative short-row knitting!

a

b

c

Evenly spaced short rows form a straight slope: a few stitches apart (a), a little farther (b), and even farther (c).

Sizing the wedges

The shapes and sizes of the wedges can vary, making for a more interesting process and garment. The distance between the wraps determines the slope of the wedge. If the wedge is wide (with many stitches), you can place the wraps far apart for a gradual slope. If the wedge is narrow (with fewer stitches), those wraps must be placed closer together and the same number of rows will create a steeper incline. A 12-stitch wedge with wraps placed 4 stitches apart can be made with 3 short-row pairs (W&T at 12, 8, and 4), while a 24-stitch wedge with wraps placed 4 stitches apart can be made with 6 pairs (W&T at 24, 20, 16, 12, 8, and 4) — and the slopes are the same!

Unevenly spaced short rows form a wave.

Vary the number of stitches between the wraps and turns to create curves or most any shape you'd like. The curved lines flow organically and are really stunning in hand-dyed yarns, as in the panel on page 67.

It doesn't really matter where you start each wedge, as long as it's balanced by a wedge at the other side of the fabric. The number of short rows can vary from wedge to wedge. I generally vary by 1 or 2 short-row pairs and use anywhere from 1 to 5 pairs for each wedge. I usually overlap short rows with those of the previous wedge to create interlocking wedges, for a sweeping line from one edge of the fabric to the other.

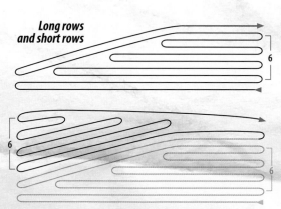

Long rows and short rows

6

6

6

Once a wedge is complete on one side, work an opposing wedge at the other side:

You can add height to a piece at any point, by working a number of full rows. To raise one side up higher than the other, complete the wedge, hide the wraps, then stack another short-row wedge above it.

Stitch patterns

Any stitch pattern can be used with creative short rows. A short-row panel can be combined with other decorative stitches: stripes, mosaic, or textures. When worked in garter, the ridges emphasize the grain of the short rows.

To create fabric that looks like intarsia, work the entire piece in stockinette. Change colors for each wedge, but continue in stockinette rather than using contrast or texture rows to delineate between the wedges.

You may choose to work garter ridges between the wedges. This is also a great place for pattern stitches or slipped stitches, since no short rows occur in this area. Full rows worked above the short rows take on the curve of the wedge below — which makes for very interesting patterning!

Yarns and colors

Each wedge provides an area in which to play with short rows and can be worked in a different color and/or yarn, as long as the gauge remains constant.

Garter ridge accents may be made with a contrast, novelty, or chunkier yarn for a few rows — it won't interfere with the overall stitch gauge.

Absolutely any fiber will work as long as you knit firmly. A loosely knit fabric will show the turns made by short rows and will look like you've made mistakes in your knitting.

Semi-solid, variegated, heathered, or marled yarns seem to hide the wraps better than solid yarns.

I love working with long-repeat yarns for creative short rows! Each wedge can begin with a different color, and the garment will look like it's made from several different yarns. Just 2 skeins offer 4 ends to start any section with, if none of those ends appeal to you, wind off yarn from the skein to find a color that does.

The simplest approach is to let a long-repeat yarn do all the work — make as large a wedge as each color allows. I often break the main skein into smaller balls of color and match them so I can control their placement, size, and shape. Experiment and do what *you* like.

Control the color: First divide a long repeat yarn into separate balls of color, then select as you knit.

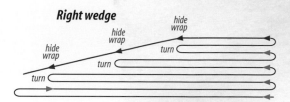

Right wedge

Short-row wraps made on RS create wedges that build up the right edge of the work.

Short rows

With short rows, we change direction and turn before the end of the row. Let's define a few points of reference:

Right side (RS) is the public side of the fabric.
Wrong side (WS) is the inside of the fabric.
Right edge is the right-hand edge of the fabric when viewed from the public side.
Left edge is the left-hand edge of the fabric when viewed from the public side.

Wrap and Turn

When making short-row turns we want to avoid leaving a hole, so at the turn we wrap the yarn around the base of the next stitch on the left needle tip. This manipulation, called **wrap and turn,** is written in the patterns as **W&T.**

The **wrap** is worked like this: Slip 1 from left needle to right needle, bring yarn between the needles to the opposite side of work (to WS if you are on a RS row, to RS if you are on a WS row), return the slipped stitch back to the left needle, return yarn between the needles to its original side of the work, then turn your piece to work the return short row. How the stitch is slipped — knitwise or purlwise — is important, but only because you don't want to end up with a twisted stitch.

Right wedges

Short-row wraps made on the RS create wedges that build up the right edge of the work.

The wrap & turn (W&T) on RS of work

Slip the next stitch knitwise to the right needle, bring the yarn to the front between the needle tips, return the stitch to the left needle so its orientation is backward (the right leg is in back), and take the yarn to the back of the work between the needle tips. Turn your piece and work back.

Notice that the wrapped stitch was NOT worked, but was just shifted from the left needle to the right needle to allow the wrap to be made, then returned to the left needle. The wrap sits at the base of that stitch, and the stitch sits on the needle in the "wrong" orientation.

The wrap at the base of the stitch causes a gap just beyond the short-row pair. Make sure, when working back on the WS, not to pull the wrap too tightly — it should have the same tension as a regular stitch.

Our illustrations show stockinette stitch, but when working seed, moss, or other stitch patterns, remember that the yarn always needs to be on the WS before making the wrap at the end of a RS short row.

Continue the W&T sequences as many times as you wish, making sure to have a few stitches between the wraps, until the wedge is the desired size. Now work a complete row, and as you come to a wrapped stitch, stop and work the wrap together with the stitch. This closes the gap and makes the short-row turns almost invisible. Take a moment and observe how this full row follows the slant of the wedge below.

Wrap and turn (W&T) on RS

1 With yarn in back, slip next stitch as if to knit. Bring yarn to front of work and return stitch to left needle, keeping its new orientation. Turn work.

2 Purl to end.

3 When you come to the wrap on a following knit row, hide the wrap by knitting it together with the stitch it wraps.

Myra's option *Lift the wrap onto the left needle and over the stitch it wrapped before knitting it together with the stitch.*

Hide the wraps

When hiding the wraps, keep in pattern — knitting or purling them together with the stitch they wrap around.

Look for the wraps, the gaps, or the stitches with the wrong orientation. Each wrap will be around the base of a stitch before the gap. I take an additional step when hiding a wrap: When I come to a wrapped stitch, I insert the right needle under the wrap, lift it over the stitch it wrapped and onto the left needle so the wrap is behind the stitch, then work the stitch together with the wrap.

With all this slipping, you don't want to end up with a twisted stitch or wrap — if you do, undo, reorient and get it right!

Left wedges

Short-row wraps made on the WS create wedges that build up the left edge of the work.

The wrap & turn (W&T) on WS of work

Slip the next stitch purlwise to the right needle, bring yarn to the back (RS of work), return the stitch to the left needle in its original orientation, bring the yarn forward (WS of work). Turn the piece and work back.

Again, the wrapped stitch was NOT worked but was just shifted from the left needle to the right needle, allowing the wrap to be made, then returned to the left needle. The wrap sits at the base of that stitch, and the stitch sits in the correct orientation. Continue the W&T sequences as many times as you wish, making sure to have a few stitches between wraps.

Hide the wraps

When I come to a wrapped stitch, I insert the right needle under the wrap on the RS of the fabric, lift it over the stitch it wrapped and onto the left needle so the wrap is to the left of the stitch, and work the stitch together with the wrap. Take care that neither the stitch nor the wrap is twisted.

Creating a rectangular fabric

A rectangle requires the same row count across the fabric, even when worked in short-row wedges. How do we work short-row wedges and match the number of rows at the left and right edges?

The easiest way is to use 2 separate row counters to keep track of the short rows — no need to count the full rows, as they will not throw the edge numbers off. Place one counter at the left edge and another at the right edge of your needle or fabric. For a right wedge, each time you work short of the left edge and back to the right edge, click the right counter twice — 1 short-row pair: 2 on right counter and 0 on left. For a left wedge, each time you work short of the right edge and back to the left edge, click the left counter twice — 1 short-row pair: 2 on left counter and 0 on right. The goal is to end the rectangle with the same number of clicks on each counter. Remember, the counters just track the short-rows at each edge; full rows are not counted.

Left wedge

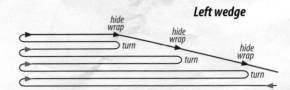

Wrap and turn (W&T) on WS

1 With yarn in front, slip next stitch as if to purl. Bring yarn to back of work and return stitch to left needle in original orientation (as shown). Turn work.

2 Knit to end.

3 When you come to the wrap on a following purl row, hide the wrap by purling it together with the stitch it wraps.

Myra's option Lift the wrap onto the left needle before purling it together with the stitch.

A bubble can fill in between wedges: Here the blue wedge is worked first, the green wedge second, and the red bubble last.

A bubble can be knit first, and the wedges filled in afterward: Work the blue bubble first, then the green wedges.

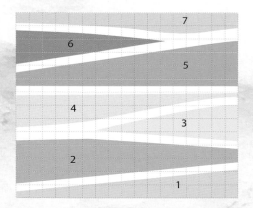

Two bubbles worked side by side.

See page 68 to enlarge the Intrepid Nomad template.

Bubbles

Let's think of the wedges as hills, and any dips between them as valleys. Bubbles fill in the valleys. **Bubbles** are short-row wedges that are placed mid-row and have both a left and right incline. They do not continue to either fabric edge, and every row (both RS and WS) gets shorter with fewer stitches before its W&T. The fabric may waver a bit as you knit, but it should block evenly. Since these short rows do not add to the height of either the right or left edge of the piece, they are not counted on either row counter.

To make the bubble shown in red Work to the top of the left wedge, wrap and turn (W&T). Work to the top of the right wedge, W&T. Work back and forth, working fewer stitches each row AND working a W&T at each row's end. The shape of the bubble depends on how many W&Ts are done. Generally, the number of wraps on each side should equal the number of wraps in its neighboring wedge so you can even out the fabric, but you can include more W&Ts to create a higher bubble, then compensate for it later. When a bubble is finished, work a row to each edge, hiding the wraps as you encounter them, making sure to work the wraps so the stitches are NEVER twisted and the wraps ALWAYS fall to the wrong side of the work.

Getting started: Instructions, charts or Freestyle? You decide!

Remember, the goal is to create a rectangular section that ends being equal in rows at both edges of the fabric. Let's review the options:

Instructions You could use the row gauge to calculate each wedge in advance and then determine the number of stitches to shift per pair of short rows. You'll then know how many stitches and rows are required within each wedge and follow that plan.

Charts You could chart the shapes with every stitch represented. If you use knitter's grid at the stitch/row ratio of your swatch, you also have a good idea of the wedge shapes. On page 63, we include a chart for the Intrepid Nomad panel.

Freestyle with a template I take a more creative journey and suggest you do the same: By having a rectangular template cut to size, I can draw wedges onto it and then play with the number of short-row pairs and turns for each section. I use the 2-counter method to keep track of my work.

I usually start with a right wedge, then work a left wedge starting just a couple stitches short of the highest W&T of the previous wedge (or short of the lowest W&T to create an opportunity for a bubble in the middle). I work wedges back and forth from one edge to the other. Between wedges, I lightly steam to my template and decide what I want to build next. I add to the side that is lower, or work a bubble if necessary. Once I've filled in a bubble, I continue to build around it. Each wedge provides an opportunity to create the next one.

This is knitting, and knitting forgives, so you'll find the number of W&Ts can vary slightly from one side to the other, while the rectangle maintains 90° corners and parallel sides. It's not necessary, therefore, to balance the number of short-row pairs in adjacent wedges. For a piece full of curves, bends, and angles, vary the number of short-row pairs from wedge to wedge. I play the numbers: 4 on the right, 6 on the left, 5 on the right, 3 on the left, and so on. Make it up as you go, and steam each wedge or bubble to the template as you complete it.

As I approach the top of the template, I total and compare the short rows at each edge. If the edges are equal, I split the area still to be knit and work the same number of short rows on each edge. If the center is low, I may knit a bubble or two. When the piece is finished, give it a good steam block and pin the corners to get nice sharp angles.

Begin at bottom of page, alternating odd-numbered wedges on left, even-numbered wedges on right.

7 Join A, work 2 rows in stockinette. ***SR 1 and 2*** Knit to last 10, W&T; purl to end. ***Next 2 SR pairs*** Knit to 15 before last wrap, W&T; purl to end. Knit 1 row, hiding wraps — 6 SR at right edge. Work 7 rows in stockinette. Cut yarn and place stitches on hold.

6 Slip 21 stitches to right needle, join A, and knit to end of row. ***SR 1 and 2*** P40, W&T; knit to end. ***Next 6 SR pairs*** Purl to 5 before last wrap, W&T; knit to end. ***Next SR*** P39, hiding wraps — 16 SR at left edge. Leave next stitch wrapped and unworked. Cut yarn; do not turn work. Slip all unworked stitches to right needle. Join B and knit 1 row, hiding remaining wrap. Knit 3 more rows. Cut yarn.

5 Join A, work 4 rows in stockinette. ***SR 1 and 2*** Knit to last 4, W&T; purl to end. ***SR 3 and 4*** Knit to 8 before last wrap, W&T; purl to end. ***Next 5 SR pairs*** On each knit row, knit to 8, then 6, then 8, then 8, then 9 before last wrap, W&T; purl to end. Knit 1 row, hiding wraps — 14 SR at right edge. Work 3 rows in stockinette. Cut yarn. Join B and knit 4 rows. Cut yarn.

4 Join A, knit 1 row. ***SR 1 and 2*** Purl to last 10, W&T; knit to end. ***Next 6 SR pairs*** Purl to 7 before last wrap, W&T; knit to end — 14 SR at left edge. Purl 1 row, hiding wraps. Cut yarn. Join B and knit 4 rows. Cut yarn.

3 ***SR 1 and 2*** Join A, k40, W&T; purl to end. ***Next 6 SR pairs*** Knit to 5 before last wrap, W&T; purl to end. ***Next SR*** K40, hiding wraps, W&T (the second wrap on this stitch); purl to end — 16 SR at right edge. Cut yarn. Join B and knit 1 row, picking up 1 wrap on Stitch 40, leave other wrap in place. Knit 3 more rows. Cut yarn.

2 Join A, work 3 rows in stockinette. ***SR 1 and 2*** Purl to last 4, W&T; knit to end. ***SR 3 and 4*** Purl to 8 before last wrap, W&T; knit to end. ***Next 5 SR pairs*** On each purl row, purl to 8, then 6, then 8, then 8, then 9 before last wrap, W&T; knit to end — 14 SR at left edge. Purl 1 row, hiding wraps. Work 2 rows in stockinette. Cut yarn. Join B and knit 4 rows. Cut yarn.

1 Knit 1 row, purl 1 row. ***SR 1 and 2*** K40, W&T; purl to end. ***Next 3 SR pairs*** Knit to 10 before last wrap, W&T; purl to end. Knit 1 row, hiding wraps — 8 SR at right edge. Purl 1 row. Cut yarn. Join B and knit 4 rows. Cut yarn.

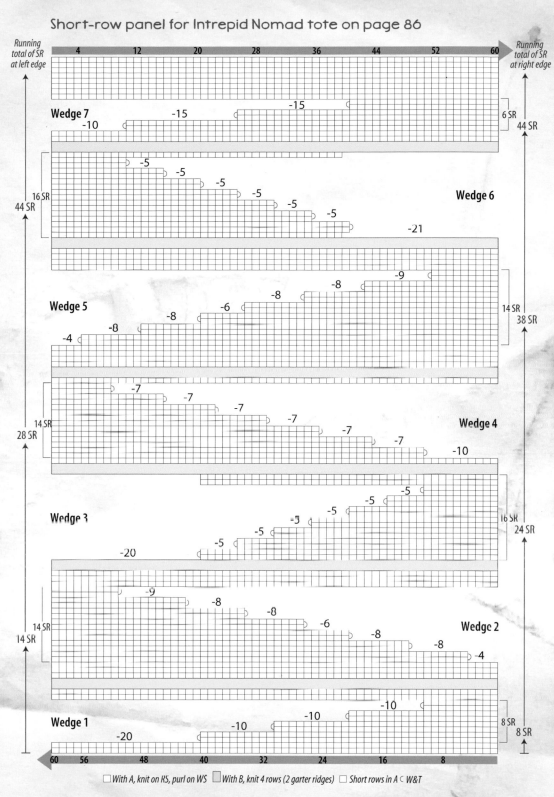

Short-row panel for Intrepid Nomad tote on page 86

Short Row Panel 1

Begin at bottom of pages, alternating odd-numbered wedges on right, even-numbered wedges on left.

GARTER RIDGE

Knit 2 rows with color of Wedge.

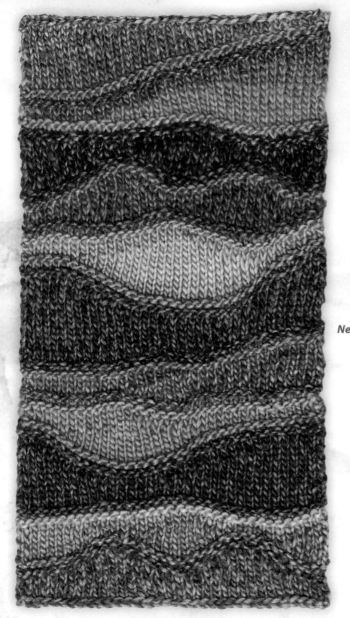

RED HEART BOUTIQUE Treasure
in color 1918 Abstract

Wedge 10

Work Garter Ridge.
SR 1 and 2 K25, W&T; purl to end.
Next 4 SR pairs Knit to 5 before last wrap, W&T; purl to end. Knit 1 row, hiding wraps —
10 SR at right edge. Purl 1 row. Knit 2 rows. Cut yarn.

Wedge 8

Work Garter Ridge.
SR 1 K15, W&T. *SR 2* P10, W&T.
Next 2 SR pairs Knit to 2 before last wrap, W&T; purl to 1 before last wrap, W&T.
SR 7 K22, hiding wraps, W&T. *SR 8* P10, W&T.
Next 2 SR pairs Knit to 2 before last wrap, W&T; purl to 1 before last wrap, W&T.
Next SR Knit to end, hiding wraps.
Purl 1 row, hiding wraps —
1 SR at right edge; 1 SR at left edge. Knit 2 rows. Cut yarn.

Wedge 6

Work Garter Ridge.
Work 3 rows in stockinette.
SR 1 and 2 P24, W&T; knit to end.
SR 3 and 4 Purl to 3 before last wrap, W&T; knit to end.
SR 5 and 6 Purl to 2 before last wrap, W&T; knit to end.
SR 7 and 8 Purl to 5 before last wrap, W&T; knit to end.
SR 9 and 10 Purl to 3 before last wrap, W&T; knit to end.
Purl 1 row, hiding wraps.
SR 11 and 12 K8, W&T; purl to end.
Next 4 SR pairs **[Knit to 2 before last wrap, W&T; purl to end. Knit to 1 before last wrap, W&T; purl to end]** twice.
Knit 1 row, hiding wraps — 10 SR at right edge and 10 SR at left edge. Knit 1 row. Cut yarn.

Wedge 4

Work Garter Ridge.
SR 1 K29, W&T. *SR 2* P14, W&T.
Next 5 SR Work to 2 before last wrap, W&T. *SR 8* P3, W&T.
Next SR Knit to end, hiding wraps.
Purl 1 row, hiding wraps —
1 SR at right edge; 1 SR at left edge. Knit 2 rows. Cut yarn.

Wedge 2

Work Garter Ridge.
SR 1 and 2 K5, W&T; purl to end.
Next 2 SR pairs Knit to 1 before last wrap, W&T; purl to end.
SR 7 K22, hiding wraps, W&T. *SR 8* P10, W&T.
Next 2 SR pairs Knit to 2 before last wrap, W&T; purl to 1 before last wrap, W&T.
Next SR Knit to end, hiding wraps.
SR 14 and 15 P10, W&T; knit to end.
Next 2 SR pairs Purl to 3 before last wrap, W&T; knit to end.
Purl 1 row, hiding wraps —
7 SR at right edge; 7 SR at left edge. Knit 2 rows. Cut yarn.

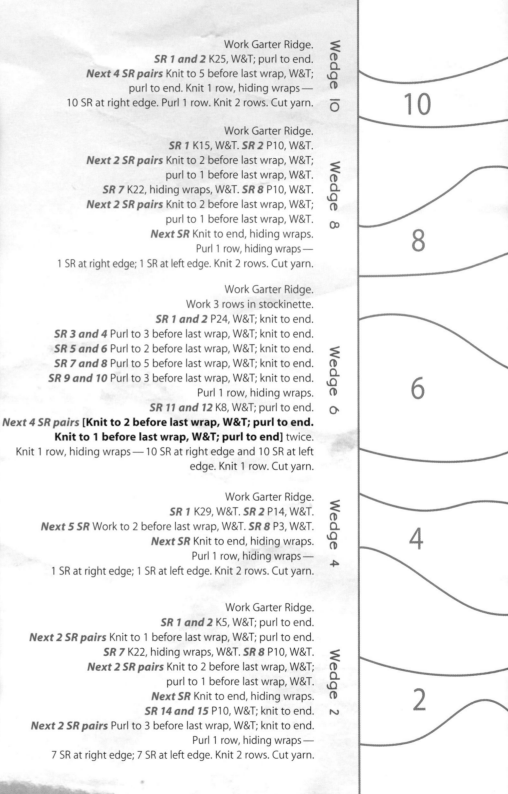

Wedge 11

Work Garter Ridge. Knit 1 row.
SR 1 and 2 P25, W&T; knit to end.
Next 4 SR pairs Purl to 5 before last wrap, W&T; knit to end.
Purl 1 row, hiding wraps — 10 SR at left edge. Bind off.

Wedge 9

Work Garter Ridge.
SR 1 and 2 K5, W&T; purl to end.
Next 2 SR pairs Knit to 1 before last wrap, W&T; purl to end.
SR 7 K22, hiding wraps, W&T. **SR 8** P10, W&T.
Next 2 SR pairs Knit to 2 before last wrap, W&T;
purl to 1 before last wrap, W&T.
Next SR Knit to end, hiding wraps.
SR 14 and 15 P10, W&T; knit to end.
Next 2 SR pairs Purl to 3 before last wrap, W&T; knit to end.
Purl 1 row, hiding wraps — 7 SR at right edge; 7 SR at left edge.
Knit 2 rows. Cut yarn.

Wedge 7

Work Garter Ridge.
SR 1 K28, W&T. **SR 2** P21, W&T.
SR 3 Knit to 3 before last wrap, W&T.
SR 4 Purl to 1 before last wrap, W&T.
Next 6 SR Work to 2 before last wrap, W&T.
Next SR Knit to end, hiding wraps.
Purl 1 row, hiding wraps — 1 SR at right edge; 1 SR at left edge.
Knit 2 rows. Cut yarn.

Wedge 5

Work Garter Ridge.
SR 1 and 2 K11, W&T; purl to end.
Next 2 SR pairs Knit to 3 before last wrap, W&T; purl to end.
SR 7 K22, hiding wraps, W&T. **SR 8** P7, W&T.
SR 9 Knit to 2 before last wrap, W&T.
Next 3 SR Work to 1 before last wrap, W&T.
Next SR Knit to end, hiding wraps.
Purl 1 row, hiding wraps — 7 SR on right edge; 1 SR on left edge.
Knit 2 rows. Cut yarn.

Wedge 3

Work Garter Ridge. Knit 1 row, purl 1 row.
SR 1 and 2 K18, W&T; purl to end.
Next 3 SR pairs Knit to 3 before last wrap, W&T; purl to end.
Knit 1 row, hiding wraps.
SR 9 and 10 P10, W&T; knit to end.
Next 3 SR pairs Purl to 2 before last wrap, W&T; knit to end.
Purl 1 row, hiding wraps — 8 SR at left edge and 8 SR at right edge.
Knit 2 rows. Cut yarn.

Wedge 1

Cast on 35.
SR 1 K15, W&T. **SR 2** P10, W&T.
Next 2 SR pairs Knit to 2 before last wrap, W&T;
purl to 1 before last wrap, W&T.
SR 7 K22, hiding wraps, W&T. **SR 8** P10, W&T.
Next 2 SR pairs Knit to 2 before last wrap, W&T;
purl to 1 before last wrap, W&T.
Next SR Knit to end, hiding wraps.
Purl 1 row, hiding wraps — 1 SR at right edge; 1 SR at left edge.
Knit 2 rows. Cut yarn.

Short Row Basics

The practice panels illustrate different and varied options available when working creative short rows. They are a great primer to help you learn how to read instructions for short rows, how to work them, and how one wedge can conform to the previous one.

Before we begin, let's set some ground rules: All odd-numbered rows are right-side rows, and all even-numbered rows are wrong-side rows.

We use the label **Row** for a full row that travels from edge to edge. As you work those rows, you may come to wraps. Always hide wraps as you come to them.

Short rows are worked in pairs. When the first row of the pair is knit, its return row is purled. When the first row of the pair is purled, its return row is knit. We use the labels **SR** for a single short row and **SR pair** for a pair of short rows.

If a line only contains a single row, it is either a full row or a partial row that completes a series of short rows and travels to the edge.

These panels are worked in stockinette with garter accents.

NOTES
See Techniques, page 120, for any unfamiliar abbreviations and techniques.

At the end of each wedge, you have a choice: Cutting gives you the opportunity to start the next wedge at a new color as shown in photo. For Panel 1, cut yarn at the end of each wedge and join from a different color of the ball. For Panel 2, you can either cut A or not.

Short Row Panel 2

Begin at bottom of pages, alternating odd-numbered wedges on right, even-numbered wedges on left.

GARTER RIDGE
Knit 2 rows (with B, for Panel 1;
with color of Wedge for Panel 2). Cut B.

NORO Kureyon in color 040 Aqua/Purple Multi (A), and MALABRIGO Merino Worsted in color 193 Jacinto (B)

Wedge 12
Work 5 rows in stockinette.
SR 1 and 2 P30, W&T; knit to end.
Next 5 SR pairs Purl to 5 before last wrap, W&T; knit to end.
Purl 1 row, hiding wraps — 12 SR at left edge.
Work Garter Ridge.

Wedge 10
Knit 1 row.
SR 1 and 2 P25, W&T; knit to end.
Next 4 SR pairs Purl to 5 before last wrap, W&T; knit to end.
Purl 1 row, hiding wraps — 10 SR at left edge.
Work Garter Ridge.

Wedge 8
Knit 1 row.
SR 1 P16, W&T. *SR 2* K11, W&T.
Next 4 SR pairs Work to 1 before last wrap, W&T.
Next SR Purl to end, hiding wraps.
Knit 1 row, hiding wraps —
1 SR at right edge; 1 SR at left edge.
Purl 1 row. Work Garter Ridge.

Wedge 6
Knit 1 row.
SR 1 and 2 P23, W&T; knit to end.
Next 2 SR pairs Purl to 8 before last wrap,
W&T; knit to end.
Purl 1 row, hiding wraps — 6 SR at left edge.
Work Garter Ridge.

Wedge 4
Knit 1 row, purl 1 row.
SR 1 and 2 K10, W&T; purl to end.
Next 2 SR pairs Knit to 2 before last wrap, W&T; purl to end.
Knit 1 row, hiding wraps.
SR 7 and 8 P15, W&T; knit to end.
Next 4 SR pairs Purl to 2 before wrap, W&T; knit to end.
Purl 1 row, hiding wraps — 6 SR at right edge; 10 SR at left edge.
Work Garter Ridge.

Wedge 2
Knit 1 row, purl 1 row.
SR 1 and 2 K18, W&T; purl to end.
SR 3 and 4 Knit to 6 before last wrap, W&T; purl to end.
Next 2 SR pairs Knit to 4 before last wrap, W&T; purl to end.
Knit 1 row, hiding wraps.
SR 9 and 10 P9, W&T; knit to end.
Next 2 SR pairs Purl to 2 before last wrap, W&T; knit to end.
Purl 1 row, hiding wraps — 8 SR at right edge; 6 SR at left edge.
Work Garter Ridge.

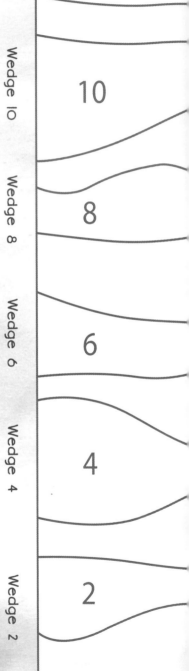

12

10

8

6

4

2

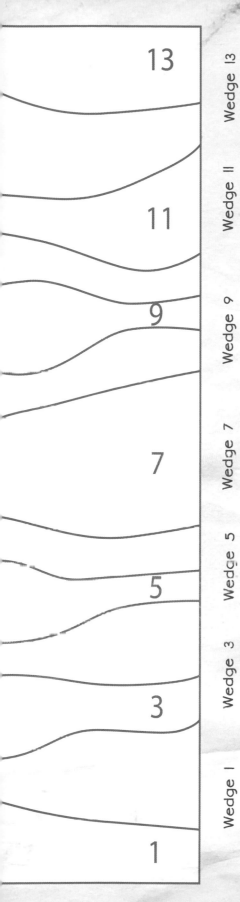

Wedge 13
SR 1 and 2 K25, W&T; purl to end.
Next 3 SR pairs Knit to 5 before last wrap, W&T; purl to end.
Knit 1 row, hiding wraps — 8 SR at right edge.
Purl 1 row. Bind off.

Wedge 11
Knit 1 row, purl 1 row.
SR 1 and 2 K10, W&T; purl to end.
Next 3 SR pairs Knit to 2 before last wrap, W&T; purl to end.
Knit 1 row, hiding wraps — 8 SR at right edge.
Purl 1 row. Work Garter Ridge.

Wedge 9
SR 1 K26, W&T. SR 2 P18, W&T.
Next 2 SR pairs Knit to 3 before last wrap, W&T;
purl to 2 before last wrap, W&T.
Next 2 SR Work to 2 before last wrap, W&T.
Next SR Knit to end, hiding wraps.
Purl 1 row, hiding wraps — 1 SR at right edge; 1 SR at left edge.
Work Garter Ridge.

Wedge 7
Work 4 rows in stockinette.
SR 1 and 2 K30, W&T; purl to end.
Next 5 SR pairs Knit to 5 before wrap, W&T; purl to end.
Knit 1 row, hiding wraps — 12 SR at right edge.
Purl 1 row. Work Garter Ridge.

Wedge 5
SR 1 K26, W&T. SR 2 P16, W&T.
Next 2 SR pairs Knit to 3 before last wrap, W&T;
purl to 2 before last wrap, W&T.
Next SR Knit to end, hiding wraps.
Purl 1 row, hiding wraps — 1 SR at right edge; 1 SR at left edge.
Work Garter Ridge.

Wedge 3
Knit 1 row.
SR 1 P25, W&T. SR 2 K15, W&T.
SR 3 Purl to 3 before last wrap, W&T.
Next 3 SR Work to 2 before last wrap, W&T.
Next SR Purl to end, hiding wraps.
Knit 1 row, hiding wraps — 1 SR at right edge; 1 SR at left edge.
Purl 1 row. Work Garter Ridge.

Wedge 1
Cast on 35.
Work 4 rows in stockinette.
SR 1 K30, W&T. SR 2 P15, W&T.
SR 3 and 4 Work to 2 before last wrap, W&T.
SR 5 K8, W&T. SR 6 P6, W&T.
Next SR Knit to end, hiding wraps. Purl 1 row, hiding wraps —
1 SR at right edge; 1 SR at left edge.
Work Garter Ridge.

Alternate Route

You can easily modify these instructions for a rectangle of a different size:

• To widen the rectangle, add stitches to the initial cast-on and continue to follow the instructions. (Just make sure that the center area has approximately the same number of rows as the 2 edges).

• To lengthen the rectangle, add plain rows of stockinette before starting the short rows for each wedge.

• To determine how many extra rows or stitches to add, you'll need to knit a gauge swatch and calculate how many more stitches or rows are needed, based on the desired size of your rectangle.

CLAUDIA HAND PAINTED YARNS
Worsted in colors Urban Fever (A) and
Copper Pennies (B)

Here's a great project for trying out creative short rows. Made as rectangles seamed at the bottom and sides, you can felt this bag for heavy wear or leave it unfelted for a larger tote. If you don't felt it, see Finish your Bag (page 114).

Exact instructions are included for the bag shown, but why not experiment with short rows in your own way? As long as you keep track of the number of rows at either edge, you can safely build wedges and bubbles. My general approach is to make one wedge, then decide what to do for the next section as I come to it, rather than mapping the whole thing out beforehand.

I've used stockinette with garter ridges, but you can use any stitch pattern you like and either include the ridges or not. Without ridges, the fabric has the appearance of intarsia. Once it's felted, the entire surface will blend together.

Easy +

Size
felted to approximately
12" x 13" x 2.5"

5.5 ▦ 3.5
1"/2.5cm over stockinette with larger needle, unfelted

Medium weight
450 total yards
(90% for A; 10% for B)

5.5mm/US9 AND
5mm/US8
60cm (24") or longer

Bag handles
fusible fleece interfacing
lining fabric and
thread to match

Notes
See Techniques, page 120, for any unfamiliar abbreviations and techniques.

To add color interest, cut the space-dyed yarn at the end of each short-row wedge, and begin the next wedge at a different place in the ball.

Intrepid Nomad Tote

Short-row panels

MAKE 2

With A and larger needle, cast on 60 stitches. Work Wedges 1–7 following instuctions on page 63.

Intrepid panel

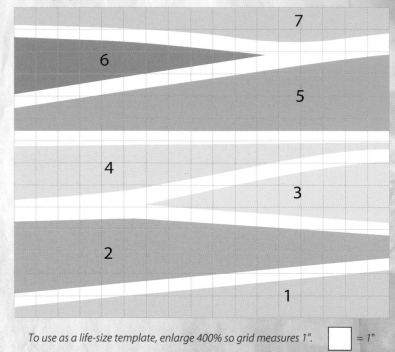

To use as a life-size template, enlarge 400% so grid measures 1". ☐ = 1"

Finishing

Block each panel to approximately 17" × 14" or to life-size template. Sew sides and cast-on edges together. Replace live stitches onto smaller needles, place marker, and join for beginning of round—120 stitches. **Rounds 1 and 3** Knit. **Rounds 2 and 4** Purl. Bind off.
Finish Paper-Bag style (page 115).
Attach handles.

Shown in NORO Kureyon in color146 (A); MALABRIGO Worsted in color 23 Pagoda (B)

Alternate Route

Use color and texture to emphasize short-rowed shapes.

MASTER TEMPLATE

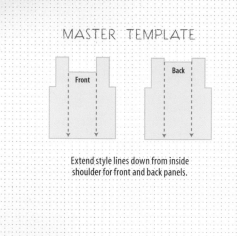

Extend style lines down from inside
shoulder for front and back panels.

Small: CASCADE YARNS Casablanca in color 04
Poppy Field (A), and KRAEMER YARNS Tatamy
Tweed DK in color Y1627 Coral (B)

Gentle waves

This long-sleeved pullover or sleeveless tank gives you a new option for the center panel of your template.

I decided to use another long color repeat for the short rows and sleeves, and a solid tweedy yarn for the contrasting color. Before starting, I split the main gradient into several balls at the color changes, to control the changes from one wedge to the next. For the sleeves I allowed the color to change and flow straight from the ball.

For the long-sleeved version I used the gradient for both front and back, but for the tank I decided to use the same short-row pattern with just the contrasting solid color on the back. Very different effects! And this helps you decide how you'd like to knit it. You could easily knit the entire top in just one color with the short rows and vertical garter-stitch panels, creating a subtle but very interesting effect.

Small: CASCADE YARNS Casablanca in color 03 Galah Cockatoo (A), and KRAEMER YARNS Tatamy Tweed DK in color Y1604 Loganberry Tweed (B)

a journey into creativity

STOCKINETTE
Knit on RS, purl on WS.

GARTER RIDGES
With B, knit 4 rows. Cut B.

RIDGE PATTERN
[Knit 1 row, purl 1 row]
twice, knit 2 rows.

I Make front SR panel

If only 2 numbers are listed, they refer to sizes 32–44 (48–52).
With larger needle and A, cast on 34 for sizes 32, 36, 40, and 44 OR cast on 38 for sizes 48 and 52.

Wedge I Work 2 (2, 2, 4, 6, 6) rows in stockinette.

SR 1 and 2 K31 (33), W&T; purl to end.

Next 2 SR pairs Work to 4 before last wrap, W&T; purl to end.

SR 7 and 8 Work to 5 before last wrap, W&T; purl to end.

SR 9 and 10 Work to 6 before last wrap, W&T; purl to end.

SR 11 and 12 Work to 3 before last wrap, W&T; purl to end. Knit 1 row, hiding wraps — 12 SR at right edge. Purl 1 row. Cut yarn. Work Garter Ridges.

Wedge 2 Join A and work 3 rows in stockinette.

SR 1 and 2 P27 (29), W&T; knit to end.

SR 3 and 4 Purl to 4 before last wrap, W&T; knit to end.

SR 5 and 6 Purl to 5 before last wrap, W&T; knit to end.

SR 7 and 8 Purl to 4 before last wrap, W&T; knit to end.

SR 9 and 10 Purl to 3 before last wrap, W&T; knit to end. Purl 1 row, hiding wraps — 10 SR at left edge. Cut yarn. Work Garter Ridges.

Intermediate

Sizes
XS (S, M, L, IX, 2X)
32 (36, 40, 44, 48, 52)"

Pick your size and make your life-size template (see page 126).

4.5   1"/2.5cm over stockinette stitch, using A and larger needle

5   1"/2.5cm over stockinette stitch, using B and smaller needle

4mm/US6 AND 3.75mm/US5, 60cm (24") or longer

crochet hook

Light weight

3

PULLOVER
900 (950, 1025, 1125, 1200, 1250) total yards as shown (60% for A; 40% for B)

SLEEVELESS
550 (575, 625, 675, 725, 775) total yards as shown (80% for A; 20% for B)

Notes
See Techniques, page 120, for unfamiliar abbreviations and techniques. Review Short Row Basics, page 58.

Cut the space-dyed yarn and begin next SR wedge with a different color.

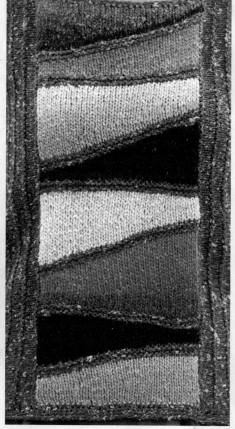

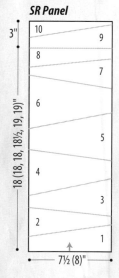

SR Panel

3"

10

9

8

7

6

5

4

3

2

1

18 (18, 18, 18½, 19, 19)"

7½ (8)"

Front Panel
Wedges 1–8
Back Panel
Wedges 1–10

Wedge 3   Join A and work 6 rows in stockinette. Continue as for Wedge 1.

Wedge 4   Join A and knit 1 row.

SR 1 and 2 P31 (33), W&T; knit to end.

SR 3 and 4 Purl to 4 before last wrap, W&T; knit to end.

SR 5 and 6 Purl to 2 before last wrap, W&T; knit to end.

SR 7 and 8 Purl to 3 before last wrap, W&T; knit to end.

Next 2 SR pairs Purl to 4 before last wrap, W&T; knit to end.

SR 13 and 14 Purl to 5 before last wrap, W&T; knit to end. Purl 1 row, hiding wraps—14 SR at left edge. Cut yarn. Work Garter Ridges.

Wedge 5   Join A and knit 1 row, purl 1 row. Continue as for Wedge 1. Work Garter Ridges.

Wedge 6   Join A and work 5 rows in stockinette.

SR 1 and 2 P31 (33), W&T; knit to end.

Next 2 SR pairs Purl to 4 before last wrap, W&T; knit to end.

SR 7 and 8 Purl to 5 before last wrap, W&T; knit to end.

SR 9 and 10 Purl to 4 before last wrap, W&T; knit to end.

SR 11 and 12 Purl to 3 before last wrap, W&T; knit to end.

SR 13 and 14 P14 (16), W&T; knit to end. Purl 1 row, hiding wraps. Knit 1 row.

SR 15 and 16 P20 (22), W&T; knit to end.

SR 17 and 18 P10 (12), W&T; knit to end. Purl 1 row, hiding wraps—18 SR at left edge. Cut yarn. Work Garter Ridges.

Wedge 7   Join A and knit 1 row, purl 1 row.

SR 1 and 2 K27 (29), W&T; purl to end.

SR 3 and 4 Knit to 4 before last wrap, W&T; purl to end.

SR 5 and 6 Knit to 5 before last wrap, W&T; purl to end.

SR 7 and 8 Knit to 4 before last wrap, W&T; purl to end.

SR 9 and 10 Knit to 3 before last wrap, W&T; purl to end. Knit 1 row, hiding wraps—10 SR at right edge. Purl 1 row. Cut yarn. Work Garter Ridges.

Wedge 8   Join A and work 3 rows in stockinette.

SR 1 and 2 P31 (33), W&T; knit to end.

SR 3 and 4 Purl to 6 before last wrap, W&T; knit to end.

SR 5 and 6 Purl to 7 before last wrap, W&T; knit to end. Purl 1 row, hiding wraps—6 SR at left edge. Work 4 (4, 4, 6, 8, 8) rows in stockinette. Bind off. Cut yarn. Steam to template.

2 Add front side panels

Left panel   With RS facing, B, and smaller needle pick up and knit (PUK) 3 stitches for every 4 rows along right edge of front SR panel from cast-on edge to bind-off, then cast on 20. Knit 1 row. Work in Ridge Pattern to shoulder width, end with a RS row. Steam to template, placing marker at bottom of armhole.

Next row Bind off to marker, then work to end of row. Work even on remaining stitches to underarm width. Steam to template. Bind off.

Right panel   Work as for left panel EXCEPT cast on 20, then PUK along left edge of SR panel from bind-off to cast-on AND bind off for armhole at beginning of a RS row. Steam to template.

3 Make back SR panel

PULLOVER   Cast on and work as for front SR panel through Wedge 8; but do not bind off. Cut yarn. Work Garter Ridges.

Wedge 9   Join A and knit 1 row, purl 1 row.

SR 1 and 2 K31 (33), W&T; purl to end.

Next 2 SR pairs Work to 4 before last wrap, W&T; purl to end.

SR 7 and 8 Work to 5 before last wrap, W&T; purl to end.

SR 9 and 10 Work to 4 before last wrap, W&T; purl to end. Knit 1 row, hiding wraps—10 SR at right edge. Cut yarn. Work Garter Ridges.

Wedge 10   Join A and work 3 rows in stockinette.

SR 1 and 2 P31 (33), W&T; knit to end.

Next 2 SR pairs Purl to 4 before last wrap, W&T; knit to end.

SR 7 and 8 Purl to 5 before last wrap, W&T; knit to end.

SR 9 and 10 Purl to 4 before last wrap, W&T; knit to end.

SR 11 and 12 Purl to 3 before last wrap, W&T; knit to end. Purl 1 row, hiding wraps—12 SR at left edge. Cut yarn. Bind off. Steam to template.

SLEEVELESS TOP   Work as for pullover EXCEPT use B throughout AND do not cut yarn between wedges.

4 Add back side panels

PULLOVER, Left panel   Turn SR panel so cast-on is at the top. With RS facing, B, and smaller needle, cast on 5, then PUK 3 stitches for every 4 rows along left edge of SR panel from cast-on to bind-off. Work as for front right panel.

Right panel   Work as for left panel EXCEPT PUK along right edge of SR panel from bind-off to cast-on, then cast on 5 AND bind off for armhole at beginning of a WS row. Steam to template.

SLEEVELESS TOP   Work as for pullover EXCEPT use B throughout AND do not cut yarn between wedges.

5 Make sleeves

With larger needle and A, work Basic Long Sleeve (page 116). With smaller needle and B, knit 4 rows, bind off, then single crochet along cuff.

Finishing

Sew shoulders and seam sleeves (page 119). With B, single crochet around neckline and hem.

SLEEVELESS TOP   With B, single crochet around armholes.

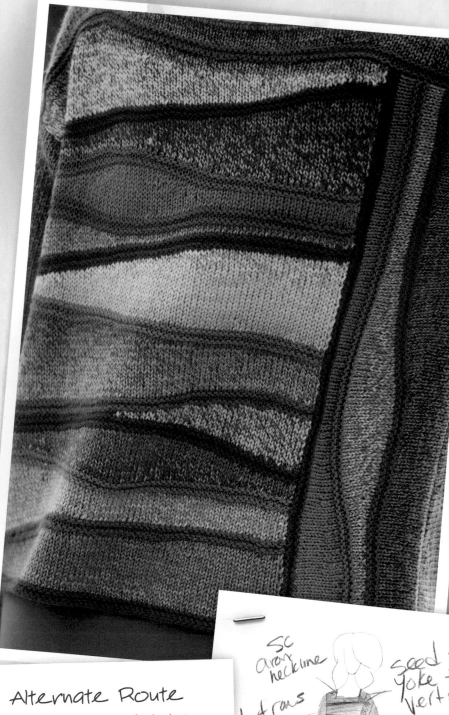

Creative short rows are so playful! Using them both horizontally and vertically creates a fantastic and bold graphic effect. Each wedge is bordered by a different accent color to add to the fun. I added a band of striping in the sleeves to allow the design to flow beyond the frame of the body.

Since the main body piece is almost a square, it's a great canvas for working short rows however you would like. Exact instructions for the pullover are included, but I encourage you to try winging it. Start with the same number of cast-on stitches and build your wedges and bubbles randomly. Just remember to keep track of how many short rows are at each edge so the row count is the same as in the sample. And as always, steam and measure as you go. Have fun!

Schematic

Back

Right Sleeve

9 (9½)"

18 (20)"

3"

5 (7)"

20½ (18½)"

Front

19"

6 (8)"   10 (11)"

5 (10)"   17"

Alternate Route

Consider other possibilities for the short-row areas. Allow the color to flow from one wedge to another. Think about playing with a different stitch pattern for each wedge. The vertical panel can be knit without short rows. Or try a stitch pattern in the yoke. How about seed stitch for the yoke and vertical panel? As long as the dimensions for each section are the same as the template, you can play all you'd like.

SC around neckline

seed st yoke + vert. panel

short rows different patterns

Stockinette

garter ridges

Sunset
Symphony

INTERMEDIATE

Sizes
S-M (L-2X)
A 44 (54)"
B 23 (24)"

1"/2.5cm over stockinette stitch
4.5

Medium weight
1225 (1500) total yards as shown (60% for A; 30% for B; small amounts of C, D, E)

4.5mm/US7
60cm (24") or longer

✛

crochet hook

Notes
See Techniques, page 120, for unfamiliar abbreviations and techniques. Review Creative Short Rows, page 58.

To change the colors in the space-dyed yarn, cut yarn at the end of each short-row wedge and begin the next wedge at a different place in the ball.

GARTER RIDGES
Knit 4 rows. Cut yarn.

Small: JOJOLAND Rhythms in colors RS64 Strawberry Sundae (A) and RS41 Radiant Orchid (B); and CASCADE YARNS Cascade 220® in colors 9605 Tiger Lily (C), 1967 Wisteria (D), and 2414 Ginger (E)

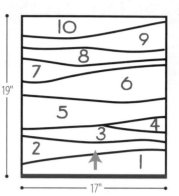

19"

17"

1 Make 2 horizontal panels

With A, cast on 78.

Wedge 1 Work in stockinette for 6 rows.
SR 1 and 2 Knit to last 8 stitches, W&T; purl to end.
Next 5 SR pairs Knit to 10 before last wrap, W&T; purl to end. Knit 1 row, hiding wraps — 12 SR at right edge. Purl 1 row. Cut yarn. With C, work Garter Ridges.

Wedge 2 With A, work in stockinette for 7 rows.
SR 1 and 2 P35, W&T; knit to end.
Next 5 SR pairs Purl to 6 before last wrap, W&T; knit to end. Purl 1 row, hiding wraps — 12 SR at left edge. Cut yarn. With D, work Garter Ridges.

Wedge 3 With A, knit 1 row.
SR 1 P62, W&T. *SR 2* K48, W&T.
SR 3 Purl to 5 before last wrap, W&T. *SR 4* Knit to 7 before last wrap, W&T.
Next 4 SR Work to 6 before last wrap, W&T. *Next SR* Purl to end, hiding wraps. Knit 1 row, hiding wraps — 1 SR at each edge. Purl 1 row. Cut yarn. With E, work Garter Ridges.

Wedge 4 *SR 1 and 2* With B, k36, W&T; purl to end.
SR 3 and 4 Knit to 6 before last wrap, W&T; purl to end.
Next 4 SR pairs Knit to 5 before last wrap, W&T; purl to end. Cut yarn.
With C, work Garter Ridges, hiding all except last wrap from first row — 12 SR at right edge. By leaving the last wrap, it will create the illusion of a sharper point.

Wedge 5 With A, work in stockinette for 9 rows.
SR 1 and 2 P64, W&T; knit to end.
Next 7 SR pairs Purl to 8 before last wrap, W&T; knit to end. Purl 1 row, hiding wraps — 16 SR at left edge. Cut yarn. With D, work Garter Ridges.

Wedge 6 With A, knit 1 row, purl 1 row.
SR 1 and 2 K60, W&T; purl to end.
Next 7 SR pairs Knit to 5 before last wrap, W&T; purl to end. Knit 1 row, hiding wraps — 16 SR at right edge. Purl 1 row. Cut yarn. With E, work Garter Ridges.

Wedge 7 With A, knit 1 row.
SR 1 and 2 P43, W&T; knit to end.
Next 6 SR pairs Purl to 5 before last wrap, W&T; knit to end. Purl 1 row, hiding wraps — 14 SR at left edge. Cut yarn. With C, work Garter Ridges.

Wedge 8 With A, knit 1 row, purl 1 row.
SR 1 K56, W&T. *SR 2* P28, W&T.
SR 3 Knit to 4 before last wrap, W&T. *SR 4* Purl to 2 before last wrap, W&T.
Next 4 SR Work to 2 before last wrap, W&T. *Next SR* Knit to end, hiding wraps. Purl 1 row, hiding wraps — 1 SR at each edge. Cut yarn. With D, work Garter Ridges.

Wedge 9 With A, knit 1 row, purl 1 row.
SR 1 and 2 K38, W&T; purl to end.
Next 3 SR pairs Knit to 10 before last wrap, W&T; purl to end.
Next SR pair K18, hiding wraps, W&T, purl to end — 10 SR at right edge.
Next SR pair Knit to 10 before last wrap, W&T; purl to end.
Next 3 SR pairs Work to 8 before last wrap, W&T; purl to end. Knit 1 row, hiding wraps — 8 more SR at right edge. Purl 1 row. Cut yarn. With E, work Garter Ridges.

Wedge 10 With A, knit 1 row.
SR 1 and 2 Purl to last 8, W&T; knit to end.
Next 6 SR pairs **[Purl to 5 before last wrap, W&T; knit to end. Purl to 5 before last wrap, W&T; knit to end. Purl to 10 before last wrap, W&T; knit to end]** twice.
Next 2 SR pairs Purl to 10 before last wrap, W&T; knit to end. Purl 1 row, hiding wraps — 18 SR at left edge. Work in stockinette for 4 rows. Bind off. Steam to schematic measurements.

2 Add vertical panels
2a Work back panel
Wedge 1 With RS of one horizontal panel facing and E, pick up and knit (PUK) 90 stitches along right edge of panel. Knit 3 rows. Cut yarn. With A, knit 1 row, purl 1 row.
SR 1 and 2 K35, W&T; purl to end.
Next 4 SR pairs Knit to 5 before last wrap, W&T; purl to end. Knit 1 row, hiding wraps — 10 SR at right edge. Purl 1 row. Cut yarn. With D, work Garter Ridges.

Wedge 2 With A, knit 1 row, purl 1 row.
SR 1 K60, W&T. *SR 2* P40, W&T.
SR 3 Knit to 5 before last wrap, W&T.
SR 4 Purl to 3 before last wrap, W&T.
Next 6 SR Work to 4 before last wrap, W&T.
Next SR Knit to end, hiding wraps. Purl 1 row, hiding wraps — 1 SR at each edge. With B, work Garter Ridges.

Wedge 3 With A, work in stockinette for 3 rows.
SR 1 and 2 P40, W&T; knit to end.
Next 2 SR pairs Purl to 5 before last wrap, W&T; knit to end.
Next 2 SR pairs Purl to 10 before last wrap, W&T; knit to end. Purl 1 row, hiding wraps — 10 SR at left edge. Work in stockinette for 10 rows.
SIZE S–M ONLY Bind off.
SIZE L–2X ONLY Repeat Wedges 1–3, then bind off.
Steam to schematic measurements.

2b Work front panel
Work as for back panel EXCEPT flip the second horizontal panel as shown, then PUK stitches along left edge.

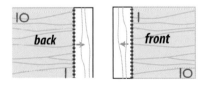

— *Cast on*
····· *Pick up and knit*
— *Bind off*
〰 *Seam*
→ *Direction of work*

3 Add yokes
3a Work front yoke
With RS facing and C, PUK104 (135) stitches along top edge of front. Knit 3 rows. Cut yarn. With B, work in stockinette for 6 (12) rows.
Divide for neck *Next row* K30 (41), bind off 44 (49) stitches, knit to end. Place first 30 (41) on hold.
Right shoulder Starting on WS, work in stockinette for 9 rows. Bind off.
Left shoulder Starting on WS, join yarn at neck and work stitches on hold as for right shoulder.
3b Work back yoke
Work as for front yoke, EXCEPT PUK along back.

4 Make sleeves
With B, cast on 82 (90). Work even in stockinette for 8 (4) rows. Dec 1 each side of next row, every 10 rows 6 (0) times, every 6 rows 9 (0) times, then every 4 rows 0 (12) times. With C, Work Garter Ridges.
Next row With A, **[Dec 1 each side of next row, work 5 rows stockinette]** twice. With D, work Garter Ridges. With A, Dec 1 each side of next row, work 5 rows stockinette. With E, work Garter Ridges. With B, Dec 1 each side every 6th row 8 times — 40 (42) stitches. Work even until piece measures 20½ (18½)".

5 Finishing
Sew shoulder seams. Measure 9 (10)" from shoulder seam down front and back and place markers. Center top edge of sleeve to body between markers and sew in place. Sew side and sleeve seams.
With B, single crochet around neckline. With B, PUK along bottom edge: 1 stitch in each stitch or garter ridge and 2 stitches in every 3 stockinette rows. With C, knit 4 rows. Bind off and seam to join.

Crazy Quilt Knitting

When you're interested in taking a slightly more challenging road to a new knitting adventure, Crazy Quilt knitting offers endless possibilities and much fun. In traditional crazy quilting, irregular shapes of fabric (often small and precious) were sewn to a foundation fabric. In Crazy Quilt knitting, shapes are sketched on a life-size template first, then each piece is knit to fit that outline. The knit pieces are joined to each other, not to foundation fabric.

Though varied, our shapes are all rectilinear — triangles, squares, rectangles, etc. — and are easy to create to size, accommodating a range of yarn sizes and gauges.

It's essential to steam block each completed piece to make sure it fits the template exactly. A hand steamer is a convenient tool to relax the fabric, straighten the edges, and set the stitches.

One more very important point: Do not stretch a piece to fit the shape. Make sure to knit each shape to just within its outline on the template so that when lightly steamed, they fit perfectly. If you stretch a piece to make it fit, it will forget — or perhaps take its revenge — and pull in when you aren't looking. This is called yarn memory — it can work for you or against you. Even if you *can* block something to the size you want, the fix is usually not permanent.

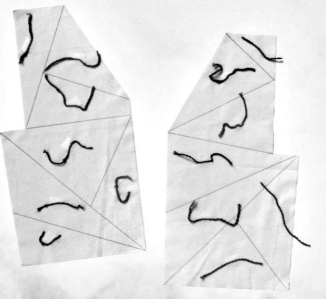

Decide on color placement before starting, by taping yarn snippets to the template.

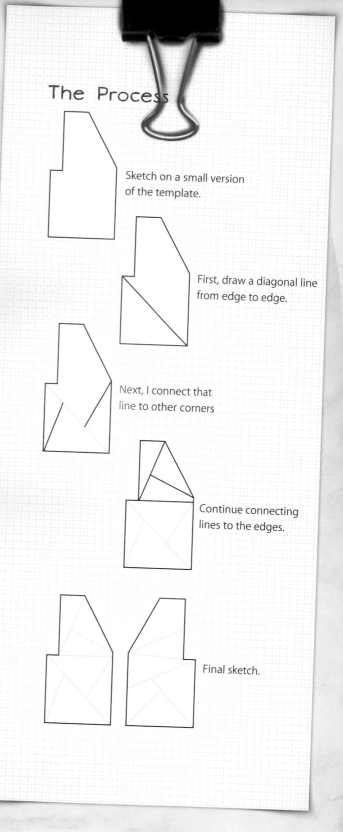

The Process

Sketch on a small version of the template.

First, draw a diagonal line from edge to edge.

Next, I connect that line to other corners

Continue connecting lines to the edges.

Final sketch.

Dividing a template into Crazy Quilt sections

The easiest templates to use for Crazy Quilt knitting are simple shapes like the ones in this book. These garments have straight edges rather than curves, so it's very easy to divide each piece into rectilinear shapes. I like to sketch on a small version of the template. Crazy Quilting is based on angles, so first draw a diagonal line from one edge of the template to another. Now find some point on that line and draw another line to a corner of the template. Continue dividing the template in this manner — connecting existing lines to the edge. Avoid triangles that measure less than 30 degrees — they are no fun to knit.

Once you like the general look on the small template, you can sketch onto the life-size muslin or Pellon template. Consider how a shape will sit on your body, and where it will look best. To minimize hips or bust, make sure you don't place the largest part of a triangle over those areas.

At this point I like to lay out the yarns in each area. Once I'm pleased with the placement, I tape small strands to the template as reminders. You don't need to decide on a specific stitch pattern until you start knitting a shape. Generally it looks best not to have the same stitch patterns next to each other, so try to vary them as much as possible. Consider simple variations like stripes, garter and stockinette combined, reverse stockinette, and seed stitch — all easy stitches to keep track of while increasing. Since I use the Modified Mattress Stitch to join the shapes, the edge stitches will not be hidden, it's usually best not to slip the first stitch of the row or create a special selvedge stitch. Work every stitch in pattern, right to the edge.

As each shape is knit and blocked, it's best to sew it right onto the existing you're creating rather than waiting until all are complete. That way, you'll be sure the final pieces fit the template perfectly — and you'll already be done with the sewing!

Make sure to measure as you knit . . .

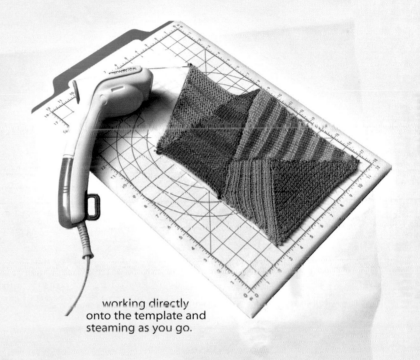

working directly onto the template and steaming as you go.

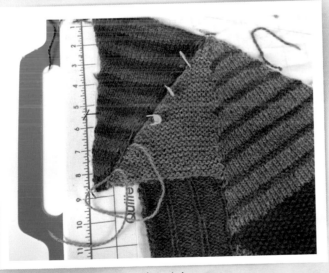

Use Modified Mattress Stitch to join pieces; pin to make sure points match.

Making the shapes

Triangles

There are 2 basic triangles I deal with for Crazy Quilt knitting: **right triangles**, where increases are made on one edge only, and **isosceles triangles**, where increases are made on both edges equally.

right triangle

isosceles triangle

Each is worked by starting at the smallest corner, casting on 1 stitch, and continuing at the suggested **rate of increase**. Measure the angle using a protractor, and refer to the Angle Chart for the closest rate of increase. Decide whether the stitch-to-row ratio is closer to stockinette or to garter stitch, and try that rate.

In some irregular triangles, the height of one side is reached before the height of the other. Work to the length of the shorter side. If the remaining wedge is slight (as shown), it may be easiest to finish it with a few short rows as you continue shaping the longer side.

If the remaining wedge is not so slight and short rows will not work, create a decrease edge using the same chart.

Once the short side (A–B) ends, a new angle needs to be figured from the B point. Draw a vertical line running perpendicular to the rows (orange line), and measure the angle between the new line and the B–D side, then refer to the Angle Chart to determine the rate of decrease for that edge (replace "increase" with "decrease"). The rate of increase for the C–D edge will continue as before.

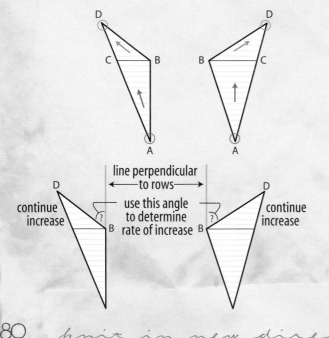

Kf&b Knit into front and back of same stitch.

Kf&b&f Knit into front, back, and front of same stitch.

It's much easier to cast on 1 stitch for a corner of a triangle and increase to the desired width than to cast on for an entire side and decrease down to 1 stitch. Check your work to the template as you knit, especially in the first couple inches of the shape. Once you're happy with the rate, you don't need to check as often, but keep your eye on the length and width to make sure it ends up the right size.

Before you begin to knit, measure the angle on the template, then check the chart for the closest rate of increase for the stitch pattern you want to use. Please note, the placement of the increases will be found in the chart, but the tension of your stitches, the size of your needles, and your yarn choice may slightly alter those rates. This is why measuring to the template is more important than sticking to the chart's suggested rate.

Steam and measure as you knit and adjust accordingly:

- To widen a triangle, increase more often.
- To narrow a triangle, increase less often.

Isosceles triangle — Increase on both ends of row.

Right triangle — Increase on 1 end only, regardless of RS or WS.

The chart gives 30°, 40° 50°, and 60° angles. Since I always increase from the smallest angle, instructions for 70° and 80° are not given.

For 35°, 45°, and 55° angles Alternate between directions for whole numbers before and after the number. For a 45° garter triangle, kf&b&f, then alternately increase 1 every 4 rows and 1 every 3 rows.

Use this same principle to combine rates for a 47° angle, etc.

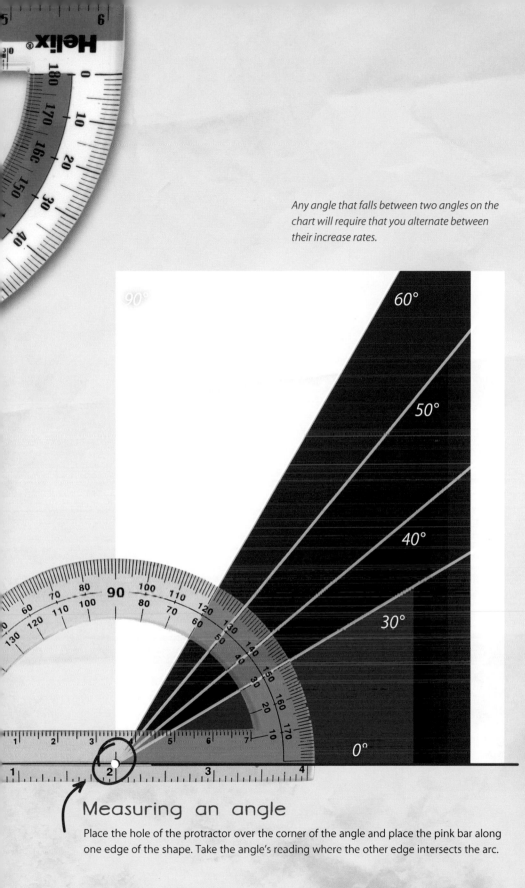

Any angle that falls between two angles on the chart will require that you alternate between their increase rates.

GARTER 1 stitch/2 rows .5 stitch/row ratio	ANGLE	STOCKINETTE 5 stitches/7 rows .71 stitch/row ratio
Kf&b, then increase 1 stitch at beginning OR end every **4** rows	30˚ 30˚	**Kf&b,** then increase 1 stitch at beginning OR end every **3** rows
Kf&b, then increase 1 stitch at beginning OR end every **4** rows	40˚ 40˚	**Kf&b,** then increase 1 stitch at beginning OR end every **2** rows
Kf&b&f, then increase 1 stitch at beginning OR end every **3** rows	50˚ 50˚	**Kf&b&f,** then increase 1 stitch at beginning OR end on 3 of every **5** rows
Kf&b&f, then increase 1 at each end every **4** rows	equailateral 60˚	**Kf&b&f,** then increase 1 at each end every **2** rows
Kf&b&f, then increase 1 at each end every **2** rows	right angle 90˚	**Kf&b&f,** then increase 1 at each end every **3** of **4** rows

30˚ 40˚ 50˚

To make a 30º, 40º, and 50º angle for an isosceles triangle, use the same rate, but alternate an increase at the beginning of the row with an increase at the end. The rows will be perpendicular to the center of the angle.

Measuring an angle

Place the hole of the protractor over the corner of the angle and place the pink bar along one edge of the shape. Take the angle's reading where the other edge intersects the arc.

Squares

Diagonal garter-stitch squares

Cast on 1 stitch. Increase at the beginning of every row until 2 sides are the desired width, then decrease at the end of every row until 1 stitch remains.

square

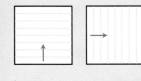

Mitered garter-stitch squares

Cast on for 2 sides + 1 stitch and mark the center stitch. Decrease 2 at the center every RS row until 3 stitches remain, then SK2P.

Center-out squares

Cast on 2 stitches for each side. Knit using any circular method, increasing 2 at each corner every other row.

Any stitch pattern can be used for knitting a square horizontally or vertically. Cast on the correct number of stitches for the repeat.

Quadrilaterals

To measure this angle, extend the lines from two sides until they meet at a point, then measure that angle as you normally would for a triangle. Cast on the number of stitches needed for the base of the four-sided shape, then continue with the rate of increase for the angle, steaming to the template as you go.

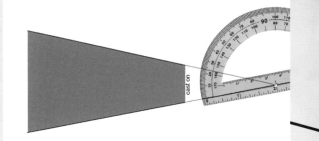

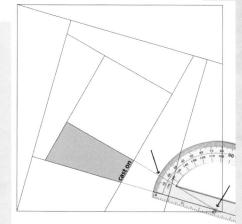

Rectangles

Rectangles are usually made by casting on for the width and working to the desired length.

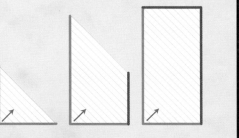

— Increase edge
— Decrease

A bias-knit rectangle in garter stitch starts the same way as the diagonal garter-stitch square, by increasing at the beginning of every row. When the desired width has been achieved, maintain the stitch count and continue the bias by decreasing 1 at the beginning and increasing 1 at the end of every row to the desired length. End the same way as the diagonal garter-stitch square, by decreasing at the end of every row.

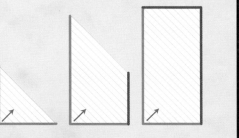

Let's start with miters

Squares Squares can be knit by increasing up or by decreasing down, or even by knitting from the center out, as for a square shawl. As long as the shape fits the template, you are free to choose.

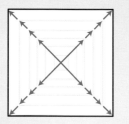 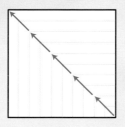

Chevrons Triangles are usually knit from the smallest angle, since it's easiest to start small and adjust as you knit, but they can also be knit from a larger angle. You may want to experiment with choosing a different starting point, especially if the patterning needs to go in a specific direction. For a different effect, consider knitting equilateral triangles as chevrons:

Cast on for the length of 1 side × 2, + 1 stitch. Mark the center stitch. On RS rows, work to 1 stitch before the marked stitch, then S2KP2. On WS rows, work even.

Rectangles Even the modest rectangle can be knit as a miter. Cast on enough stitches for 2 mitered squares, then decrease at each "square's" center.

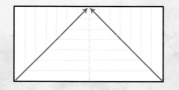

Short-row turns

Another use for short rows is to establish the angles at the ends of a parallelogram. Determine the width of the piece and multiply by the stitch gauge for the cast-on number. Begin at one end and knit short-row pairs until the knit rows are perpendicular to the parallelogram's sides. Knit full rows until one side ends, then work more short rows as needed to complete the shape. Our illustration shows a right short-row wedge at the beginning and a left short-row wedge at the end.

Calculate how many short-row pairs you'll need by measuring the height needed to establish a 90° angle with the sides, then multiply that measurement by the row gauge. Divide by 2 to see how many pairs of short rows you'll need. I generally work 2 pairs, then measure to my template to see how many more I need to do.

Alternate Route

Each of the shapes shown here indicate a direction of knitting. Based on a a particular stitch pattern or the need for stripes to go the opposite way, you may decide to knit them differently. I'm including a few alternatives, but don't stop there! You always have the option to knit shapes from another direction.

Trekking triangles

Intermediate

Sizes

XS (S, M, L, 1X, 2X)

32 (36, 40, 44, 48, 52)"

Pick your size and make your life-size template.

8 ▦ 5.5 — 1"/2.5cm over stockinette stitch

4mm/US6
60cm (24") or longer
AND
needle 1 or 2 sizes smaller for ribbing

③ Light weight
825 (875, 950, 1025, 1100, 1150) total yds as shown

Notes

See Techniques, page 120, for any unfamiliar abbreviations or techniques.

Review making the shapes on page 80.

Make sleeves

Work Basic Long Sleeve or Short Sleeve (page 116) changing color as desired and ending with a RS row.

Cuff Change to ribbing needle and color. Purl 1 row. Work K2, P2 Rib for 2", changing color after 4 rows for short sleeve. Bind off in pattern.

Finish your cardi

Steam all pieces to template. Sew shoulders and seam sleeves (page 119).

Bottom band With RS facing, desired color, and ribbing needle, pick up and knit (PUK) stitches along bottom edge of fronts and back, adjusting stitch count to a multiple of 4 + 2 on next row if necessary. Work K2, P2 Rib for 2". Bind off in pattern.

Front band Mark right front for 5 buttonholes, with the first ½" from the beginning of neck shaping, the last 1" from the bottom, and the rest spaced evenly between. With RS facing, desired color, and ribbing needle, PUK along right front, across back neck, and down left front. Work Seed Stitch for 1½" AND on 6th row, work yo k2tog at each buttonhole marker. Bind off. Embellish with embroidery stitches between pieces and between color changes as desired.

The cropped cardi is the perfect canvas for Crazy Quilt knitting. My theme for filling in the shapes was stripes, using different textures and colors. Some are 1 color with garter ridges; in others, 2 colors create the stripes. The fun part is deciding as you start each shape what you want the stripe pattern to be—all garter ridges, stockinette with garter ridges, or garter with stockinette breaks. Once a pattern is established, just continue until the shape is the right size, then bind off.

First make the crazy pieces

I include the stitch patterns I used for each area, but feel free to mix it up any way you'd like. Any yarn from sport-to-worsted weight will work, and different fibers are fine.

Crazy pieces continue on page 86.

Small: ROWAN Baby Merino Silk DK in colors 681 Zinc, 677 Teal, 678 Rose, 679 Clay, and 672 Dawn

Embroidery

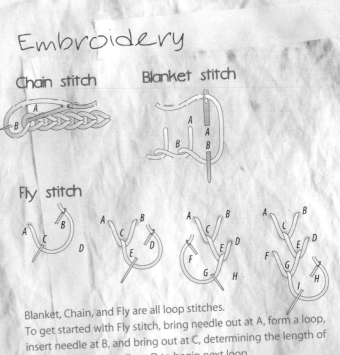

Chain stitch   **Blanket stitch**

Fly stitch

Blanket, Chain, and Fly are all loop stitches.
To get started with Fly stitch, bring needle out at A, form a loop, insert needle at B, and bring out at C, determining the length of the stitch. Insert needle at D to begin next loop.

→ direction of work
— increase along this edge
— recalculate for decrease
   for irregular triangles or
   quadrilateral shapes
— begin CO more than 1 stitch

Right front

a Alternate 2 Garter Ridges in 1 color, 1 Garter Ridge in another color.

b Alternate 6 stockinette rows in 1 color, 6 rows in another color.

c Cast on required number of stitches for edge closest to center front, then work in Seed Stitch in 1 color.

d Alternate 6 stockinette rows in 1 color, 1 Garter Ridge in another color.

e Alternate 6 Garter Ridges in 1 color, 4 stockinette rows in another color.

f Stockinette in 1 color.

g Garter in 1 color.

Left front

h Alternate 1 Garter Ridge in 1 color, 1 Garter Ridge in another color OR Double Seed in 1 color.

h2 SIZES L–2X ONLY Seed Stitch in 1 color.

j Alternate 5 Garter Ridges in 1 color, 4 stockinette rows in another color.

k Alternate 8 stockinette rows, 8 reverse stockinette rows in the same color.

l Alternate 4 stockinette rows in 1 color, 4 rows in another color.

l2 SIZES M–2X ONLY Garter in 1 color OR work as for h.

m Garter in 1 color.

n K2, P2 Rib in 1 color.

Crazy pieces

Work pieces separately, steam to template, then sew together.

Shape C is actually a quadrilateral shape, not a triangle. Measure the width for the smallest side and multiply by stitch gauge for the cast-on. Draw lines on your schematic to extend each side until they meet, then use your protractor to measure that angle (see page 80). Cast on the required number of stitches and proceed with that angle's rate of increase.

Shape O has several options for starting. The arrow indicates starting at the lower right corner and increasing until the width of the rectangle is achieved, then working even until it's the proper length. But you could also knit it from the top down and decrease at the same rate. A third option is to measure the width of the rectangle and cast on the number of stitches needed, do 2 to 3 short row pairs to fill the angled portion then continue working full rows for the desired length.

Back

o Work as for k.

p K6, p1 rib in 1 color. Flip piece over for reverse stockinette.

q Alternate 6 Garter Ridges in 1 color, 6 Garter Ridges in another color.

r Seed Stitch in 1 color.

s Work as for d.

t Garter in 1 color.

u Work as for b.

v Garter in 1 color.

w Alternate 6 Garter Ridges in 1 color, 6 stockinette rows in another color OR 5 Garter Ridges, 4 stockinette rows.

x Stockinette in 1 color.

y SIZES M–2X ONLY Garter in 1 color.

DOUBLE SEED STITCH

MULTIPLE OF 4

Row 1 (RS) [K2, p2] to end.

WS rows Knit the knit stitches
and purl the purl stitches.

Row 3 [P2, k2] to end.

K2, P2 RIB *MULTIPLE OF 4 + 2*

RS rows [K2, p2] to last 2 stitches, k2.

WS rows [P2, k2] to last 2 stitches, p2.

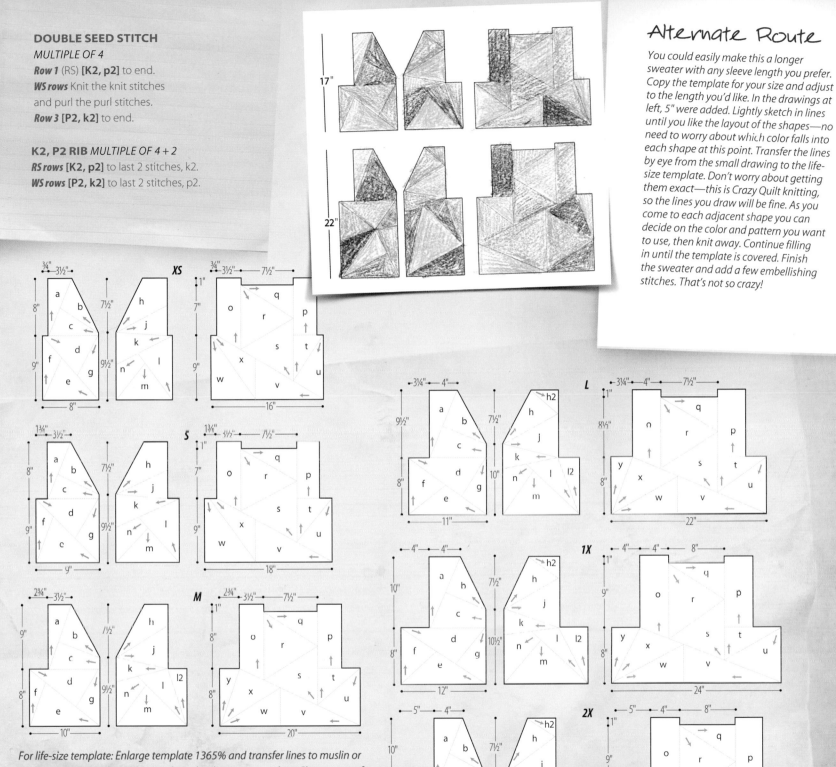

Alternate Route

You could easily make this a longer
sweater with any sleeve length you prefer.
Copy the template for your size and adjust
to the length you'd like. In the drawings at
left, 5" were added. Lightly sketch in lines
until you like the layout of the shapes—no
need to worry about which color falls into
each shape at this point. Transfer the lines
by eye from the small drawing to the life-
size template. Don't worry about getting
them exact—this is Crazy Quilt knitting,
so the lines you draw will be fine. As you
come to each adjacent shape you can
decide on the color and pattern you want
to use, then knit away. Continue filling
in until the template is covered. Finish
the sweater and add a few embellishing
stitches. That's not so crazy!

For life-size template: Enlarge template 1365% and transfer lines to muslin or
Pellon. Measure each starting angle and indicate on template. Choose yarns for
each area and tape a strand in the section as a reminder.

Small: Short-sleeved version: CASCADE YARNS Cascade 220®
Sport in colors 2452 Turtle, 2450 Mystic Purple, 9451 Lake
Chelan Heather, 4010 Straw, 2453 Pumpkin Spice, and 9456
Sapphire Heather

a journey into creativity → → →

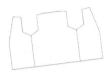

Merging lanes

By using one piece for this vest, I have a lot of ground to cover with crazy-quilt shapes. I always start with a small paper template and lightly pencil in lines until I'm happy with all the angles. Then I transfer them to a life-size fabric template, approximating the same angles. The great thing about redrawing the lines onto the fabric is that they don't have to be perfect, since I know I'll just knit whatever angle ends up on the template. From there, it's working each shape, steaming, and filling in until the entire template is covered—almost like doing a jigsaw puzzle.

I chose another long-repeat yarn that I broke into small balls so it looked like many different colors of the same type of yarn. This allowed me to make sure no adjacent shapes were the same color—and it gave me lots of choices to play with. Can you believe this is just one colorway?

Since the nature of crazy-quilt knitting in stockinette is to pucker slightly, make sure to steam each piece and all the joins well so that they lie flat. You are also free to mix in other stitch patterns, or to knit each shape in garter or seed stitch instead.

Alternate Route

If you prefer more of a flare at the hemline, templates can be split apart to include an additional wedge as illustrated below. Cut the original template at each side seam and swing the front to add flare. If you'd like an additional 4" in the vest, pivot each front from the underarm point to create a 2" gap at the hemline.

Then what? One option is to knit the entire new inset piece as one shape (below left). Or you can redraw shapes across the main body to include the new area (below right).

Another alternative is to isolate the Crazy Quilt knitting to the fronts and back, with the sides knit in another stitch pattern (above). This could also be a way to increase width at the hemline with short rows in the side pieces.

1 Start anywhere you'd like. Knit the largest shapes first, then fill in with adjustment shapes, always knitting to fit the template.

2 Pin edges and use a tail to do a Modified Mattress-Stitch join.

3 Separate colors from the long-repeat ball and position them on the template to balance the design.

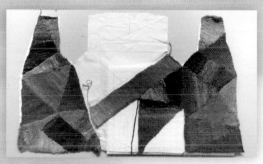

4 Continue to fill in the template until it's covered, making sure to stitch pieces together as you finish them.

I used a gauge of
3 1/2 stitches
and 6 rows to 1"

On 5.5mm/US9 circular needle
60cm (24") or longer

and approximately
650 (675, 725, 800, 875, 900)
total yards.

Allow extra yardage if
controlling color in a long-
repeat multi-color yarn.

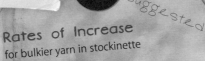

Suggested

Rates of Increase
for bulkier yarn in stockinette

Kf&b then:

Angle	Increase
20°	+1 every 4 rows
30°	+1 every 3 rows
45°	+1 every 2 rows
60°	+2 every 3 rows

Start small

First, review the introduction to Crazy Quilt knitting starting on page 78. Although triangles can be knit in any direction, it's easier to adjust the rate of increase if you start from the narrowest angle. Look at each triangle and find that corner. For stockinette stitch, use M1R and M1L increases.

Often, one side of the triangle is slightly longer than another. When you reach the height of the shorter side, work short rows as needed to reach the height of the longer side, then bind off.

Steam with care

If you are using yarn with acrylic content, knit a triangle and steam it to see how it will grow. If after blocking it is wider than desired, try the instructions for an angle that's 10° smaller. Regardless of the fiber content of the yarn, make sure to frequently compare the shape to the template as you knit.

Join as you go

Use your best judgment when joining the shapes. If you're joining a bound-off edge to a side edge, you may want to mattress stitch just inside the bind-off to hide the ridge. If you join *into* the edge as in Modified Mattress Stitch, the bind-off will show as a decorative line.

Finish simply

Sew shoulder seams. Pick up stitches at the hem and knit several rows, then pick up evenly around the front and neck edge and knit several rows for a garter-stitch trim see Pick-up Rates, page 118). You can substitute several rows of half double crochet if you'd prefer.

Single crochet evenly around the armholes.

Small, on page 89: NORO Kureyon in color 219 and ARAUCANIA Nature Wool in color 20
Above: RED HEART BOUTIQUE Treasure in color 1919 Watercolors

4"   15½"   10"

11"

12½"   2X

13"   26"   13"

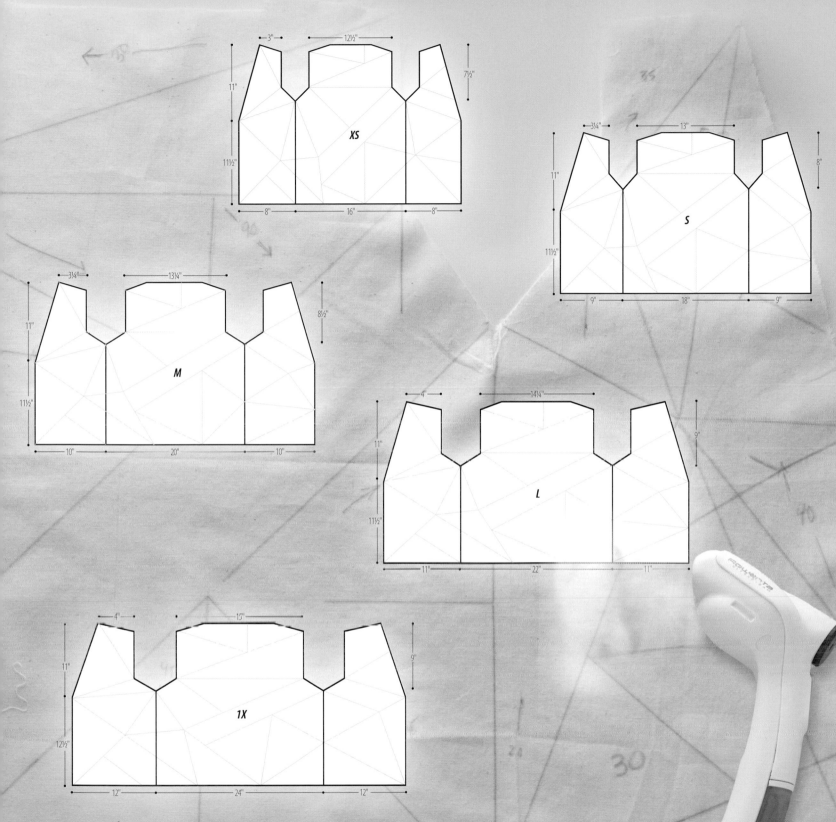

For life-size template: Enlarge template 1375% and transfer lines to muslin or Pellon. Measure each starting angle and indicate on template. Choose yarns for each area and tape a strand in the section as a reminder.

Freeform Knitting

If you are ready to take your knitting completely off road, Freeform is the way to go! This totally template-based approach is multidirectional and doesn't depend on gauge.

Unlike Crazy Quilt knitting, in which the shapes are mapped out on the template before you cast on the first stitch, in Freeform knitting the life-size template is a blank piece of muslin or Pellon. The entire template is yours to roam around in however you like — Freeform is free range. It's also an opportunity to be as creative as you like with only one restriction — the template must be completely filled in, with no overlapping pieces. The goal is to achieve a fabric that lies flat and just fits the template. How you go about it is your choice.

I'll take you through my process for *Higher Ground*, my blue jacket, and I also include patterns — although a pattern for Freeform is almost an oxymoron — to show several ways to include Freeform knitting in garment construction. *Follow the Rainbow*, page 100, plays within blocks. In *Joyful Journey*, page 104, linear shapes divide a rectangle horizontally and vertically. For *Southwestern Splendor*, page 108, I place shapes diagonally, then fill in the remaining areas.

Once you understand the overall approach, I encourage you to play! However you fill in the template is valid.

Mix stitch patterns, techniques, and yarns — you've most likely done that already!

Work with different needle sizes and gauges — it's easier than you think.

Make use of your other skills and fiber interests — add crochet, weaving, or beads.

This is the method to *my* madness. Soon you'll develop your own methods.

Freeform is all about "What happens if. . .?" While working, ask yourself, "What if I do this?" or, "What if I try that?" And don't stop there! Do it, try it, see what happens, and you have your answer.

And remember: In Freeform, there is no "wrong!"

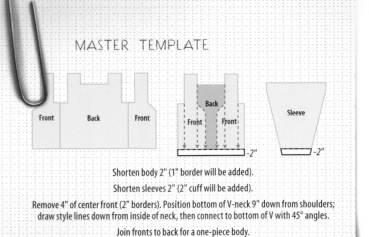

Front   Back   Front

Back
Front Front

Sleeve

-2"   -2"

Shorten body 2" (1" border will be added).

Shorten sleeves 2" (2" cuff will be added).

Remove 4" of center front (2" borders). Position bottom of V-neck 9" down from shoulders; draw style lines down from inside of neck, then connect to bottom of V with 45° angles.

Join fronts to back for a one-piece body.

Higher ground

Template Pick your size and make your life-size template of fabric or Pellon (see page 126), then make the style adjustments shown here.

Yardage Check the Approximate Yardages on page 125 for the yardage to allow for your size, using the gauge you will be using. For example, a sweater such as this one with a gauge of 6 stitches and 9 rows in stockinette suggests 1450 yards (9 skeins of Koigu); I will add 2 skeins to allow for the garter ridges and 1 or 2 more skeins for the frequent color changes within the modular shapes. Check the yardage on the ball band and see how many balls or skeins you'll need, then divide that into as many colors as you'd like. My estimate of 13 skeins allows me to have up to 12 different colors plus I added 3 more of 1 color for the bands and trim.

Theme Before starting a Freeform project, I pick a general theme. For Higher Ground I chose linear shapes with garter ridge patterns, using 1–3 colors per element. I was able to create a fabric with a very complex look just by changing the number of rows between stockinette and garter ridges, or changing the colors for each multiple of rows. The combos I used were:

3 garter ridges, 2 rows stockinette;

3 garter ridges, 3 rows stockinette;

1 garter ridge, 2 rows stockinette;

2 garter ridges, 6 rows stockinette.

After knitting a few pieces and placing them into the template, I decided to incorporate repeats of **[k2, slip 2 with yarn to WS]** into a few bands to add a spark of contrast.

Shapes and techniques I used Mitered squares and triangles, slip-stitch patterns, bias knitting, Crazy Quilt triangles, and creative short rows.

Small: KOIGU YARNS
KPPPM in 12 colors

"Think of the template as the overall map to your final destination, but there are unlimited routes."

3 As a piece is made, I pin it in place then join to adjacent shapes using Modified Mattress Stitch.

I Starting with my favorite palette and a scrumptious yarn always helps.

2 Once the life-size template is cut, start filling in. I like to attach the template to a large piece of cardboard so that it's easy to turn it and move it around as I work.

Allow your knitting to evolve. Start by creating a number of larger modular pieces, lay them on the template at different angles, and let your knitting tell you what to do next.

I usually wait until the entire piece has been assembled, try it on, and then decide what the edgings should be. Of course I have already left room for these additions.

This is a fluid process. You are not following a set-in-stone plan.

Steaming is a gentle process. When we steam, we are not stretching or distorting the fabric. The steam allows it to relax into the shape it will assume naturally after washing and wearing—perhaps with a bit of patting.

My general approach is to create the largest pieces first without knowing in advance exactly what they will be. I find it works best if there are 3 large elements that relate to each other in different areas, maybe on the back and each front. I place them on the template and rearrange the shapes until I feel a comfortable balance. Since I love combining ridges and colors in mitered squares, I may start by making 3 large mitered squares—completely different but related in color. Once I'm happy with an arrangement, I draw lines that extend from their sides out to the edges of the template. Nothing is written in stone, but this gives me a general direction for how I want the knitting to evolve.

I can pick up along the edges of the squares I have made, or knit new pieces and join them with Modified Mattress Stitch. As the template fills in, I decide where and what to knit next. And I still may move pieces around—even if it means undoing a join or two. Feel free to change your mind as much as you'd like.

As the template fills in, specific shapes need to be knit to fit all the way to the edge. These last pieces are always knit to exact sizes as fill-ins. I find it easiest to knit the small pieces separately, steaming and measuring to the template as I knit.

After the template has been completely covered, it's time to pin the fabric down at the corners and along the edges and steam block it, straightening out any kinks in the edges. You can wet block at this point, but I find a good steaming usually does the trick.

Once all the pieces are blocked to size, the garment is ready for finishing (see page 119).

A Slip-stitch Corrugated Rib is my favorite way to finish off—combining some texture, 2 colors, and a little bit of pattern. It ties everything together like a mat and picture frame—but choose any border technique you like.

SLIP-STITCH CORRUGATED RIB
MULTIPLE OF 4 + 2
Slip stitches with yarn on WS.
Row 1 (RS) With A, **[k2, sl 2]** to last 2 stitches, k2.
Row 2 (WS) With A, **[p2, sl 2]** to last 2 stitches, p2.
Row 3 (RS) With B, **[sl 2, k2]** to last 2 stitches, sl 2.
Row 4 (WS) With B, **[sl 2, p2]** to last 2 stitches, sl 2.

SOME THOUGHTS WHILE WORKING:
Stitches

I like to use stitch patterns that are garter-based or that combine knit and garter stitches fairly evenly, like seed or moss. Because we are knitting in different directions, stockinette fabric may have a tendency to bulge once it hangs upright, even if it lies perfectly flat on the template. Textured stitches help avoid this. Including even a few rows of garter will work better than a full area of stockinette.

Feel the flow of the knitting. Start with the basic concepts—rate of increase, number of stitches to cast on, how many rows to knit—but allow yourself to adapt as you knit.

By being aware that you are measuring the knitting to the template while you work and by watching how it evolves, you will fill even complex spaces without having to adhere to a set of rules. Imagine you are taking a walk with your knitting and following different paths. Wander this way and that and see what happens. Introduce new colors or shapes whenever you want. Turn around and go the other way. Maybe turn the whole thing upside down!

5 Body template . . .

4 Close-up of joins.

6 . . . and sleeve templates completely filled in.

This type of knitting expands your awareness. By being present with the knitting, working one stitch or one repeat at a time, and breathing, you may even experience a sense of lightness and peace—an added benefit!

As you measure and steam to the template as you work, make sure to keep the fabric completely flat—no bulges. This doesn't mean you can't use textured stitches—use them whenever you want! Just make sure that, when steamed, they relax and lie perfectly flat without rippling. Check to your template frequently so if you need to frog, it will only be a few rows.

Get into the habit of joining each piece with a length of the tail right after it's finished. Even though we are joining at the very edge, the fabric will contract a bit from the Modified Mattress Stitch. You'll often need to adjust the next shape to accommodate the new fabric that's been created. If you wait until several pieces have been completed, you may find they no longer fit the template perfectly.

When you come close to the edges of the template, it's crucial that you check your work every other row or so. I generally work on a lapboard with my T-pins and hand steamer close by. This makes it very easy to check the progress and carefully judge how to proceed. You may find a couple of short rows are all that's needed to fit to an edge. Do whatever you need to so that the bind-off fits the template perfectly, without overlapping or coming up short. Avoid stretching the knitting more than about ¼", because the fabric will want to return to its original shape—even after a good blocking.

Freeform knitting takes time. Embrace this! There are no bonus points or gold stars for being fast. One project may take weeks, months, or more. While this seems like a long time to invest in one sweater, as my husband often reminds me, "You'd be knitting anyway."

7 With a one-piece body, the Freeform shapes flow seamlessly from front to back.

a journey into creativity →→→ 95

Awesome Odyssey

This Freeform carrying pouch can be made to fit any zippered pouch. I love the mesh make-up bags from beauty supply shops, but any zippered pouch with a smooth surface and a cloth zipper tape will work fine.

The challenge

Make squares, rectangles, and triangles, using at least 2 colors in each shape.

What you need

A zippered pouch to cover
Muslin or Pellon for a template
5 or more colors of yarn that work well together, all the same weight
Circular knitting needle and crochet hook
Sewing needle and thread.

SHORT-ROW RECTANGLE

OVER 16 STITCHES
Cast on 16.
WEDGE: SR 1 and 2 Work 15, W&T; work to end.
Next SR pair Work to 3 before last wrap, W&T; work to end.
Next 4 SR pairs [Work to 3 before last wrap, W&T; work to end. Work to 2 before last wrap, W&T; work to end] twice.
Work 1 row, hiding wraps. Change color and knit 2 rows. Work an odd number of wedges for an angled end, an even number for a square end.

After finding the bag you want to cover, make a template from muslin or Pellon the exact shape and size of the rectangle you'll need to create as the covering. The knitting will wrap around the bottom of your pouch.

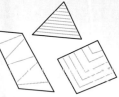

Now you are free to fill in the template any way you'd like! Start with some larger shapes, the short-row panel, triangles, or squares, which can also do double duty as a gauge swatch.

Arrange them onto the template, then draw lines from the sides of the shapes to the edges of the template to create triangles, rectangles, and squares to fill it in the rest of the way. Make sure the entire template is covered, with no overlapping edges of knitting. Steam each piece as it is finished. Decide as you knit a piece whether to pick up along a previous edge or to cast on and join it to the adjoining shape using Modified Mattress Stitch.

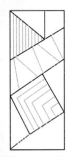

Fold the rectangle in half. I like to steam block it right onto the pouch and adjust the corners and edges if needed, then mattress stitch the sides closed. Remove the zipper bag and single crochet around the top edge of your knitting to even it out. Slip the zipper bag back in and carefully hem stitch the top edge of the single crochet to where the zipper joins the bag. Add a zipper pull if you'd like. There you go—a perfectly lined, zippered pouch to hold anything you can think of!

Use your favorites

Try any Freeform knitting techniques, like mitered squares, slip-stitch and other patterns, stripes and ridges, creative short rows, bias knitting, modular pieces.

For more on pouch-style finishing, see page 114.

Uncommon avenues

This simple rectangle uses a linear Freeform approach. Folded envelope style, it creates a safe place for delicate items on the go.

You can cut a template to any size rectangle you'd like. Decide how large you want the bag to be, double it and add several inches for a fold-down flap. Cut a piece of muslin or Pellon that size.

You can easily sketch lines on 1-inch grid paper to decide how to break up the sections and then transfer the lines to your template, or you can just knit sections and fill in the template, making sure to steam as you go.

I mirrored the front and back, knitting two identical pieces and then flipping them on either side of a center strip. Once that rectangle was composed, I picked up stitches and knit a long strip to fill in the template.

This bag offers lots of opportunities to try different color combinations and mixed techniques. Simple stripes mixed with mitered pieces and triangles add to the overall effect. Try combining sections of different stitch patterns, too!

I ♡ my iPad case!

SKACEL/HIKOO
Simpliworsted in colors
15 Ripe Raspberry (A),
55 Burnt Orange (B),
059 Simply Sage (C),
and 63 Amber Waves (D)

SEED STITCH

Row 1 Sl 1 purlwise wyif, **[k1, p1]** to last 2 stitches, k2tog.

All remaining rows Sl 1 wyif, **[knit the purl stitches and purl the knit stitches]** to last 2 stitches, k2tog.

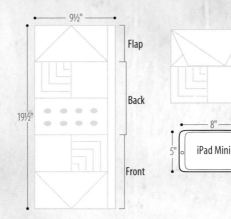

Make your panel

Schematic shows cast-on, bind-off, pick-up edges, and direction of knitting. Pick up with RS facing. Steam blocks to 3½" or 7" square as you work them.

a With A, cast on 31. Mark center stitch with a removable marker. **All RS rows** Knit to 1 before marked stitch, S2KP2, knit to end—2 stitches decreased.

Work in colors and stitches as follows:

[With A, knit 4 rows; with C, knit 1 row, purl 1 row] twice. With A, knit 4 rows. With D, knit all rows until 3 stitches remain. SK2P, cut yarn, and fasten off.

b With B, pick up and knit (PUK) 15 from right edge of **a**.

Rows 1, 3, 4, and 6 **[K3, p3]** to last 3 stitches, k3.
Rows 2 and 5 **[P3, k3]** to last 3 stitches, p3.
Repeat Rows 1–6 three times, binding off in pattern on Row 6.

c With C, pick up 31 from bottom of one of the **a/b** rectangles. Knit 3 rows.
Row 4 (RS) With D, knit.
Row 5 Purl.
Row 6 With A, **[k2, sl 2 wyib]** to last stitch, k1.
Row 7 K1, **[k2, sl 2 wyif]** to last 2 stitches, k2.
Repeat Rows 4–7 three times, then knit 1 row, purl 1 row. With C, knit 4 rows. Bind off, leaving tail for seaming.

d With C, pick up 31 from top of **a/b**. Work in Seed Stitch until 2 stitches remain, k2tog.

e *MAKE 2* With B, cast on 1, kf&b&f—3 stitches.
All rows Knit to last 2 stitches, kf&b, k1.
Alternate 2 rows B and D until triangle fits template—approximately 23 stitches.
Bind off and stitch to sides of **d**.
Make another panel of **a**, **b**, **d**, and **e**.
Turn remaining panel 180 degrees and mattress stitch to **c**. Steam to 7" X 18".

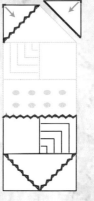

f With C, pick up 74 across long side of rectangle. Knit 3 rows; cut yarn. Join B, work 4 rows in stockinette; do not cut yarn. Join D, **[k2, sl 2 wyib]** to last 2 stitches, k2.
Next WS row **[K2, sl 2 wyif]** to last 2 stitches, k2. Cut yarn. With D, work 4 rows in stockinette, cut yarn. With C, knit 4 rows. Bind off.

Edging With C, pick up stitches and knit 4 rows. Bind off. Repeat along other 3 sides of rectangle.

Finish your bag

Steam to 9½" × 19½".
Finish envelope-style (page 114).

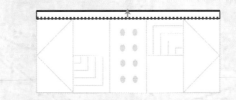

Follow the Rainbow

This creative top can use as many different techniques and stitches as you'd like! Since it's based on squares and rectangles, each section can be treated as an independent portion of knitting. You are welcome to follow the "map" I've set out for you or substitute your own techniques in each section. The dimensions for each area are given — as long as you knit to that size you can do anything you'd like. I used a wonderful long-repeat colorway and started at different points in the ball. The finished piece looks like it was made from different balls of yarn.

Some of the shapes can be picked up easily from an adjacent shape, but others may be easier to knit separately and sew onto the main fabric — it's totally up to you. The advantage of sewing? The shapes can be moved around or rotated 90, 180, or 270 degrees, then sewn together. The advantage of picking up stitches? No sewing! I use a combination of the two, finding that some pieces will lie flatter when knit separately and sewn together.

The most important thing to note is that the finished shapes all have 90-degree angles, regardless of needle size or yarn. Not all the yarns have to be the same, as long as they're all the same weight. Explore mixing needle sizes and yarns, too. Some stitches, like slipped stitches and stranded work, have a tendency to draw in — add a few more stitches to the cast-on or go up a needle size to remedy this. Generally, textured patterns that combine knit and purl stitches drape better than stockinette — I still like to mix in a little stockinette break now and then in areas like short rows.

GARTER SLIP-STITCH BLOCKS *MULTIPLE OF 4 + 1*

Slip all stitches purlwise, with yarn to WS of work.
A1 and A2 refer to two colors of yarn A. See Note 2.
With A1, cast on or pick up 33 stitches.
Purl 1 row, knit 1 row, purl 1 row, do not cut yarn.
RS rows 4 and 8 With A2, **[k2, slip 2]** to last stitch, k1.
WS rows 5 and 9 K1, **[slip 2, k2]** to end.
Row 6 With A1, k1, slip 1, **[k2, slip 2]** to last 3 stitches, k3.
Row 7 K1, p2, **[slip 2, p2]** to last 2 stitches, slip 1, k1.
Rows 10–13 With A1, work in stockinette, carrying A2 up the side. Repeat Rows 4–13, cutting A2 after Row 9.

MITERED SQUARE

Cast on and/or pick up and knit (PUK) stitches as directed.
Mark center stitch. Knit 1 row (WS).
RS rows Work to 1 stitch before marked stitch, S2KP2, work to end — 2 stitches decreased.
WS rows Either knit or purl across. The square should be at least 75% garter, but you can place 2–3 stockinette breaks whenever you'd like.
When 1 stitch remains, cut yarn and fasten off. Steam.

WAFFLE STITCH *MULTIPLE OF 3*

Rows 1 and 3 [K2, p1] to end.
Row 2 [K1, p2] to end.
Row 4 Knit.
Repeat Rows 1–4.

Waffle stitch

FLAME STITCH *MULTIPLE OF 8*

All WS rows Knit the knit stitches and purl the purl stitches.
Row 1 [K1, p7] to end.
Row 3 [K2, p5, k1] to end.
Row 5 [K3, p3, k2] to end.
Row 7 [K4, p1, k3] to end.
Row 9 [P1, k7] to end.
Row 11 [P2, k5, p1] to end.
Row 13 [P3, k3, p2] to end.
Row 15 [P4, k1, p3] to end.
Repeat Rows 1–16.

Flame stitch

☐ Knit on RS, purl on WS
☐ Purl on RS, knit on WS

intermediate

Sizes
S/M (L/1X)
48 (54)"

8.5 1"/2.5cm over garter stitch using smaller needle
4.5

Medium weight
1175 (1425) total yards as shown
(90% in A and 10% in B)

4mm/US6
4.5mm/US7
60cm (24") or longer
AND
spare needle for 3-needle bind-off

crochet hook
removable stitch markers
waste yarn

Notes
See Techniques, page 120 for any unfamiliar abbreviations or techniques.

If you choose to select specific colors, you'll need 13 extra balls. Otherwise, allow the colors to flow straight from the ball and start each square from a different end.

Small: NORO Silk Garden Lite in color 2079 (A) and CLAUDIA HAND PAINTED YARNS Worsted in Marooned (B)

Make panel I

Schematic shows cast-on, bind-off, and pick-up edges, and direction of knitting. Pick up with RS facing. Use smaller needles unless otherwise indicated. Steam blocks to 3½" or 7" square as you work them.

a Cast on 33. Work Mitered Square. Steam to 3½".

b Pick up and knit (PUK) 16 along edge of **a**, cast on 17 — 33 stitches. Work Mitered Square.

c Cast on 17, PUK32 along edge **a/b**, cast on 17 — 66 stitches. Knit 1 row. Place markers on stitches 17 and 33. Work as for Mitered Square EXCEPT work S2KP2 before each marker — 4 stitches decreased — AND when 6 stitches remain, S2KP2 twice. ***Next WS row*** SSK, cut yarn, and fasten off.

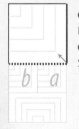

d Cast on 33 then PUK32 along edge **a/b**. Work Mitered Square.

e With larger needle, PUK33 along edge of **d**. Work Garter Slip-stitch Blocks. Do not cut A1.

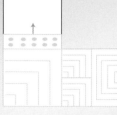

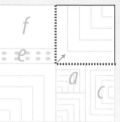

f With smaller needle, knit to last 2 stitches, k2tog — 32 stitches. Purl 1 row. ***Begin Flame Stitch*** Work Rows 1–16, then Rows 1–8. Bind off.

g PUK33 along edge **a/c** and 32 along edge **e/f**. Work Mitered Square.

h Join as you go. (If you prefer, you can create a separate 7" diagonal square and sew it to **f**). Turn work so **d** is in lower left corner. PUK1 from top right corner of **f**, turn, kf&b, turn, k2, PUK1 from **f**. ***WS rows*** Knit to next to last stitch, kf&b, k1. ***RS rows*** Knit to end of row, PUK1 from **f**. Continue until 32 stitches are picked-up from edge. ***Next row*** Knit to last 2 stitches, k2tog. Repeat last row until 1 stitch remains. Cut yarn and fasten off.

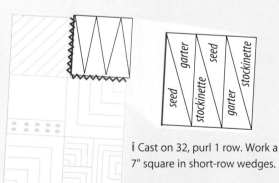

i Cast on 32, purl 1 row. Work a 7" square in short-row wedges.

Each wedge can be a different stitch pattern. Always start a new wedge with 1 plain row of knitting, then begin stitch pattern.

WEDGE *SR 1 and 2* Work 30, W&T; work to end. ***Next 5 SR pairs*** Work to 5 before last wrap, W&T; work to end. Work 1 row, hiding wraps — 12 SR at wedge edge. Work 1 row — 1 wedge complete. Work 1 row to begin next wedge.
Repeat for a total of 6 wedges. Bind off. Steam to 7" square and sew in place.

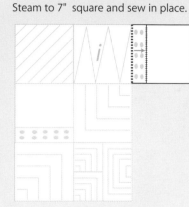

j With larger needle and A, PUK33 along edge of **i**. Work in Garter Slip-stitch Blocks.

k With smaller needle and new color, knit 2 rows. Work Rows 1–4 of Waffle Stitch 6 times.

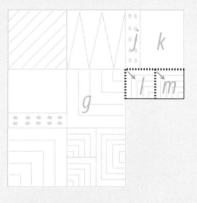

l Mark center of remaining edge **g** and adjoining edge **j/k**. PUK16 from marker on **g** to corner, PUK1 in corner, PUK16 from corner of **j** to marker on **j/k** — 33 stitches. Work Mitered Square.

m PUK16 along edge of **l**, PUK1 in corner, PUK16 along remaining **k** edge. Work Mitered Square.

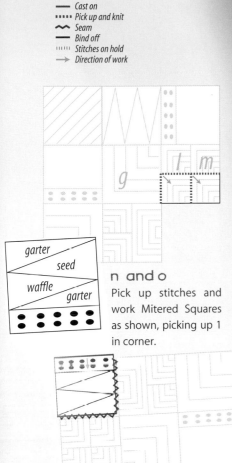

n and o
Pick up stitches and work Mitered Squares as shown, picking up 1 in corner.

p With larger needle, cast on 33 and work Garter Slip-stitch Blocks. Do not cut yarn.

q With smaller needle, work 4 short-row (SR) wedges as follows:

WEDGE **SR 1 and 2** Work 30, W&T; work to end. **Next 4 SR pairs** Work to 5 before last wrap, W&T; work to end. Work 1 row, hiding wraps — 10 SR at wedge edge. Work 1 row — 1 wedge complete. Work 1 row to begin next wedge.
Repeat for a total of 4 wedges. Bind off. Steam to 7" square and sew in place. Steam entire panel to 21" square.

Make panel 2

Now it's time to make another panel, and it's decision time: Repeat Panel 1, make Panel 2, or create your own combination of 7" squares. Have fun!

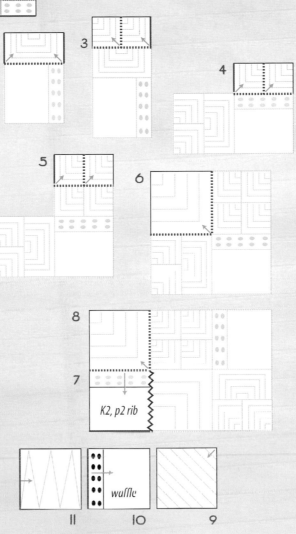

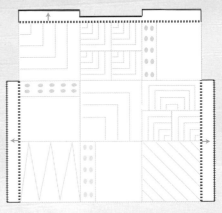

Now it's time to decide which panel is the front and which is the back and their orientation.

Add the yoke

Front yoke With smaller needle and B, PUK32 across each square along top edge of front panel — 96 stitches. Knit 1 row. Work one 4-row repeat of Waffle Stitch. **Next row** Work 33, bind off next 30 stitches for neck, work to end. Place first 33 stitches on hold.

Right shoulder Continue in pattern for 4 more repeats, working last Row 4 in purl. Bind off.

Left shoulder Join yarn on WS of stitches on hold, then work as for right shoulder.

Back yoke Work as for front yoke EXCEPT work three 4 row repeats before binding off for neckline AND work two more repeats before binding off for shoulder.

Add underarm panels

With RS facing and B, PUK33 along each of 2 lower squares — 66 stitches. Knit 1 row. Complete two (four) 4-row repeats of Waffle Stitch ending with a purl row instead of a knit row. Place stitches on hold. Repeat along other side.

Finish your top

Sew shoulder seams. With RS together, place held side stitches on needles and join using 3-needle bind-off.
Single crochet around neck.
Single crochet 1 round, then half double crochet around armholes and bottom edge.

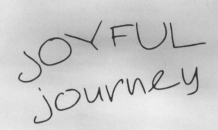

JOYFUL journey

This sweater offers you the opportunity to play within a specified shape—a rectangle. It's easy to fit linear shapes into your template, using your yarn and your gauge.

On pages 106 and 107, you'll see details for my Freeform panels, but I encourage you to experiment and allow yours to evolve.

To begin, pick coordinating colors of yarn in the same weight, and colored pencils to match. Using the master templates on page 126, trace, photocopy, or draw a small version of your size. Color in areas for an overall idea of color balance. You don't need to worry about specific shapes or techniques yet.

I like to pick a theme that will run through the whole garment. This sweater is worked with variations on squares and triangles. You'll be amazed at how many different techniques you can use.

There are style decisions you will make in the sketching stage: I included a border on each side of the main panels, so needed to allow for that on the template.

First, make the Freeform panels

Since the yoke and sides are picked up and knit onto the Freeform panels, you fill in the front and back templates first. I treated the back as two columns and each front as one column, but you can divide up each panel any way you like.

Freeform panels continue on page 106.

Small: BERROCO Ultra Alpaca Light in colors 4283 Lavender Mix (A), 4294 Turquoise Mix (B), 42104 Briny Deep (C), and 4275 Pea Soup Mix (D)

knit in new directions

Add underarm panels

You have a choice: You can knit the underarm panels separately and sew them onto the front, or pick up the required number of stitches along the sides of the front and back panels and knit them sideways. This is an easy way to create vertical garter ridge stripes that flatter and that provide an easy place to insert short rows for A-line shaping. Check the schematic and mark the bottom of the armholes, calculate how many stitches to pick up by multiplying the length of the panel from underarm to hem by the stitch gauge, then pick up stitches between underarms and hem. Work to the width needed for your size, then bind off, OR put stitches on hold and join the sides using a 3-needle bind-off.

Make sleeves

Work Basic Long Sleeve on page 116.

Finish your cardi

Steam all pieces to the template. Sew shoulders and seam sleeves (page 119).

Front bands, neckline, and hem edges are up to you! At this point I like to try the sweater on and decide what technique I'll use for the finishing. I choose buttons and decide how many to use before I figure out the placement of the buttonholes. I prefer to single crochet and then half double crochet around the neckline. Mark each inner corner and decrease 2 to 3 stitches there every row for a sharp turn. Next I knit the hem by picking up stitches evenly across the bottom, check the Pick-up Rates on page 118.

The front bands are last, and are picked up along the front edges between the top of the neckline edging and the bottom of the hem band. Since not all the pieces from the Freeform panels will be side edges, take care when picking up the stitches to avoid rippling or puckering. I start with the left band since it has no buttonholes, and match the count for the other side. After a few rows, hit it with a little steam and see how it lies. If you need to adjust the band, it's better to rip out now than to find out it's too small or too large after you have knit the entire band. Mark the right front for buttonholes, then work yo-k2tog at each marker when working the right band.

Sizes
XS (S, M, L, IX, 2X)
32 (36, 40, 44, 48, 52)"

Pick your size and make your life-size template (see page 126)

10
5
1"/2.5cm over garter stitch

3

Light weight
1250 (1300, 1425, 1575, 1675, 1750) total yards as shown

+

stitch markers
crochet hook

3.75mm/US5
60cm (24") or longer

Intermediate

PYRAMID STITCH

Row 1 (RS) [P5, k1] to end.
Row 2 [P2, k3, p1] to end.
Row 3 [K2, p1, k3] to end.
Row 4 [K3, p1, k2] to end.
Row 5 [P1, k3, p2] to end.
Row 6 [K1, p5] to end.
Repeat Rows 1–6.

Stitch key
☐ K on RS, p on WS
▨ P on RS, k on WS

6-st repeat

Freeform panels

I like to knit a shape, place it into the template, and then decide what the next shape will be. As I get ready to knit the next piece, I draw in the lines so I can knit to the template. Try to balance the colors and make sure not to position two shapes of the same color next to each other. Use all the colors and experiment with techniques: mitered squares, slip-stitch patterns, triangles, and different stitch patterns.

After filling in everything but the side borders, I steam the rectangles, pick up stitches along the long edges, and knit a simple slip-stitch pattern to finish filling in the panel.

Now it's time to add the yoke.

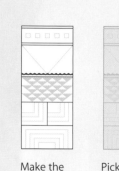

Make the Freeform panels.

Pick up and knit to fill template.

Pick up and add yoke.

Pick up and add underarm panels.

~ Seam
→ Direction of work

Right Front   **Left Front**

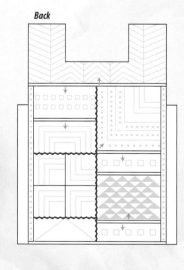

Back

Work center triangle: in stockinette (R front), garter (L front), garter stripe (back).

Work edge triangles in stockinette and sew together.

Work 4 mitered squares in 1, 2, 3, 4 sequence to avoid seaming. (See page 83 for general instructions).

Large mitered square worked with k2tog-yo rows for eyelets, and garter slip stitch with a contrast color.
On RS with CC, **[sl 1, k1]** to center dec, **[k1, sl 1]** to end. On WS, slip the slipped stitches and knit the knit stitches.

Mitered rectangle— see page 83.

2 bands of 2-stitch garter blocks over 10 rows.

3-stitch garter blocks over 6 rows.

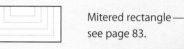

1 Pyramid Stitch block.

Add the yoke

Each yoke is picked up and knit from the top edge of a Freeform panel using a zigzag stitch pattern. Use your template, calculate how many stitches need to be picked up by multiplying the width of the yoke by your stitch gauge. I like to jot this number onto my small schematic. Then calculate how many rows you will knit by multiplying the height of the yoke to the neckline, by the row gauge. Again, write down how many rows are needed. At the neckline, you'll bind off stitches to create the square edge. Multiply the number of inches for the neck bind-off by the stitch gauge, then multiply the number of inches you need from the neckline to the top of the shoulder by the row gauge to see how many more rows you'll knit to the top of the shoulder. Make sure to maintain the stitch pattern after binding off for the neckline. Steam the fronts and the back to the schematic.

Now it's time to add underarm panels.

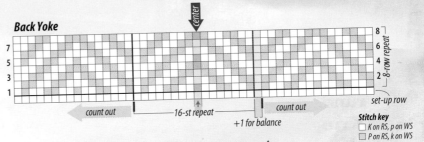

Back Yoke

count out — 16-st repeat — +1 for balance — count out — set-up row

Stitch key
☐ K on RS, p on WS
☐ P on RS, k on WS

Centering a large repeat

For the back

With RS facing and B, pick up and knit an odd number of stitches. Knit 3 rows.

a Count stitches on needle   _____

b Find closest odd number of 16-st repeats that you can subtract from total   − _____

c Subtract and you have $a - b =$ _____

d Subtract 1 (balance stitch) $c - 1 =$ _____

e Divide that number by 2 $d \div 2 =$ _____

f Go to Yoke chart and count that number outward from each red marker and mark on chart:

At right, label the mark *BEGINNING OF BACK AND LEFT FRONT.*
At left, label the mark *END OF BACK AND RIGHT FRONT.*
With RS facing, change to A and knit 1 row. Work Yoke chart between your marks for back yoke, following template and calculations for neck and shoulders.

For the right front

With RS facing and B, pick up and knit across right panel. Knit 3 rows. **Set-up row** (RS) With A, knit across. **Next row** (WS) Work Row 1 from the mark labeled *END OF RIGHT FRONT,* and when row is complete mark chart for final stitch of that row (to the right of center repeat). Label the mark *BEGINNING OF RIGHT FRONT.* Work Chart between your RF labels, following template and calculations for neck and shoulder.

For the left front

Count the number of stitches between *BEGINNING OF RIGHT FRONT* mark and red mark. Count the same number of stitches to the left of the red mark at left and place mark on chart and label *END OF LEFT FRONT.* With RS facing and B, pick up and knit the same number of stitches on left front as for right front. Knit 3 rows. **Next row** (RS) With A, knit across. **Next row** (WS) Work Row 1 of Yoke chart between Beg of LF and end of LF. Continue shaping reversing as for right front yoke.

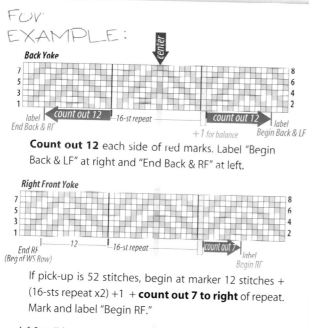

FOR EXAMPLE:

Back Yoke

count out 12 — 16-st repeat — count out 12
+1 for balance
label End Back & RF — label Begin Back & LF

Count out 12 each side of red marks. Label "Begin Back & LF" at right and "End Back & RF" at left.

Right Front Yoke

End RF (Beg of WS Row) — 12 — 16-st repeat — count out 7 — label Begin RF

If pick-up is 52 stitches, begin at marker 12 stitches + (16-sts repeat x2) +1 + **count out 7 to right** of repeat. Mark and label "Begin RF."

Left Front Yoke

label End LF — count out 7 — 16-st repeat — 12 — Begin LF

Count out 7 to left of repeat. Mark & label "Begin LF."

Clearly you only need 1 chart.
If you had picked up 53, count out 8!

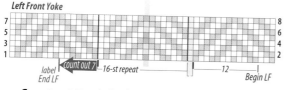

MASTER TEMPLATE

Extend style lines down from shoulders for front and back panels. Allow 1" at center front for front band. 7" down from front shoulders draw 45° lines to front band for v-neck.

Southwestern splendor

I'm hoping by now you feel brave and empowered enough to venture out on your own! I will explain all of the steps that I took to achieve the final garment, but I want you to think about it as an approach rather than specific instructions.

Once your life-sized template is cut out of muslin or Pellon, you can use it to lay out the pieces you knit in any order you like. With a template I can compare my knitting to the size I need to knit to at any moment—I won't wander too far astray. The other wonderful thing about this approach is that you are free to work on any portion you want at any time. Maybe you want to work on several mitered squares one evening. Each square can be placed and moved until you're happy with the arrangement, then the areas around it can be filled in as needed.

I begin by choosing the yarns—in this case, one gorgeous variegated yarn from Fiesta Yarns and several solid colors.

I print out a small template and pencil in lines to establish the panels I need for each area. Using colored pencils, I sketch in the basic plan based on the yarn colors, indicating the way I plan to fill in each area.

Next it's time to swatch to determine the needle size to use, and to be able to calculate the stitches and rows per inch. I try different stitch patterns and steam well to see how the fabric will drape.

Next I transfer my pencil lines onto the life-size muslin or Pellon template.

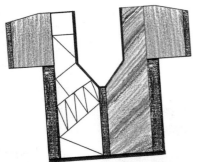

Small: FIESTA YARNS Boomerang in colors 3166 Peacock, 3952 Chaco Canyon, 3908 Salmon Run, 3946 Cilantro, and 3915 Grape Skin; Gelato in color 3166 Peacock

RIDGE PATTERN

[Knit 1 row, purl 1 row] 3 times, knit 2 rows. Repeat last 8 rows.

DEC 1

At beginning of row SSK.
At end of row Work to last 2 stitches, k2tog.

INC 1

At beginning of row Kf&b in first stitch.
At end of row Kf&b in next to last stitch.

Begin back Freeform panel with a mitered square and a short-row strip. Fill in with a couple of triangles.

NOW IT'S TIME TO KNIT!

I decided to knit the bias panels first. Your measurements will vary, but the method is exactly the same. You don't have to work the garter ridges, or you can do the bias panels in garter stitch — it's totally up to you!

Make the bias panels

Right back panel

a Work increase section

With B, cast on 1, kf&b&f—3 stitches. Work in Garter Ridge pattern and AT SAME TIME, Inc 1 at beginning and end on 3 of every 4 rows until bottom edge matches width of template shoulder.

b Work straight section

Continue in pattern and AT SAME TIME, Inc 1 at beginning and Dec 1 at end of every RS row until longest side matches template.

c Work decrease section

Dec 1 at beginning and end on 3 of every 4 rows until 3 stitches remain. SK2P. Cut yarn and fasten off.

Left back panel

Work as for right-side panel EXCEPT Dec 1 at beginning and Inc 1 at end of RS rows for straight section.

Left front panel

Work increase section as for back right-side panel until bottom matches width of template. Work straight section until shortest side matches template, end with a RS row. *Next WS row* Lay front on your template and mark inner edge of neck opening with removable marker. Bind off to marker. Continue on remaining stitches as for back panel.

Add underarm panels

Block front and back panels to template, placing marker at bottom of armhole. Pick up stitches between marker and hem for the stitch pattern you want to use — I chose Double Seed Stitch (see page 87) . Knit to underarm width. Steam to template. Bind off.

Make the Freeform panels

Rather than determining exactly what I will knit to fit the space, I first make several mitered squares to fit diagonally in the panel, using the gauge to determine how many stitches to cast on, changing my yarns every few rows, and throwing in slipped stitches on a couple of rows. Once the squares are done and lightly steamed, I lay them into the template and draw lines that extend to the edges of the panel, forming triangles. I also draw in lines for a rectangle to be filled in with creative short rows. Before I knit a new shape, I measure its angle or width and either check the angle chart for its rate of increase or cast on the number of stitches needed for the width of, say, the short-row rectangle.

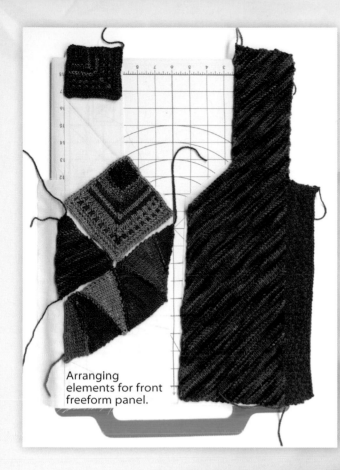

Arranging elements for front freeform panel.

CORRUGATED RIB
MULTIPLE OF 4 + 2
All RS rows [K2A, p2B] to last 2 stitches, k2A.
All WS rows [P2A, k2B] to last 2 stitches, p2A.

As each piece is completed and steamed, I use Modified Mattress Stitch to join it to the adjacent shape. Once the entire panel is filled in, I steam it to the template to make sure it fits.

Make the sleeves

Work Basic Short Sleeve (page 117) in Ridge Pattern, using a contrast color for the ridges. I worked a band of Double Seed Stitch to match the Underarm panels (see page 87).

Finish your jacket

I use the same basic method of finishing for most of my garments. I join the shoulder seams, lay the front and back pieces out with RS up, and place the sleeves in the armholes, making sure to line up the center of the sleeve with the shoulder seam. I seam the sleeves to the body, then fold the garment at the shoulder seams, match and pin the sides and underarms, and sew the seams, starting at the underarm and working toward each hem. At this point the whole sweater gets a good steam block.

To finish this cardi, I pick-up stitches evenly along the hem of the body and knit 3 garter ridges, then single crochet around the neckline. For the front plackets, I use Corrugated Rib with simple yo-k2tog buttonholes on the right front, sew on the buttons, and am ready to wear my finished piece!

Tools, techniques, & templates

a journey into creativity → → →

Finish your bag

To get started with creative knitting, you may want to start simply with a rectangular template and fill it in with whichever method you'd like. Once complete, the knit panel can become a piece of a garment, or better yet, a bag, with just a little added finishing.

Knits stretch, and a knit bag often needs to be stabilized — either by adding a lining or by fulling it for a more rugged knit. The options are endless — you can make a tote, a small purse, or even an outer layer that wraps around an existing zipper pouch. All you need is a template in the appropriate dimensions.

For a bag that requires a lining, use a traditional lining fabric or a coordinating cotton print for a fun surprise when the bag is open — check out the pink leopard print inside *Uncommon Avenues!*

Should you decide to cover a pre-made bag or pouch with knitted fabric, add ½" on all sides to your template for seams. Knit the fabric that will cover the template, seam it and slip it over the pre-made pouch, then stitch with matching upholstery thread. (*Awesome Odyssey*)

Fulling/Felting your knit bag

Should you decide that you don't want to line a bag, fulling is the answer. I will only full the knitting when the finished look is more about the color than the texture. I find that fulled fabric obliterates the stitch definition and blurs the lines between color changes, so I save that process for times when I need something sturdy and the look will not be compromised.

Remember that fulling will shrink your knit, so you will want to make your template larger. And don't invest in fancy stitches that will disappear in the process — just stick to stockinette or garter and let the color do the talking. Remember that different yarns shrink differently, so just watch your knitting as it is being felted in the washer. Also, only animal fiber or animal fiber blends will felt. If you are unsure, test first.

Carry on

I like to scour antique and thrift shops for bags with interesting handles (*Radiant Rainbow Bag*) and often repurpose the handles by sewing them onto knitted bags. Twisted cords made out of the yarns in the bag are also nice, keeping the interest on the knitting. Little treasures like a great buckle, button, or bead might just be the perfect accent.

TOTE STYLE

There are just a few easy steps to creating a bag with a lining:

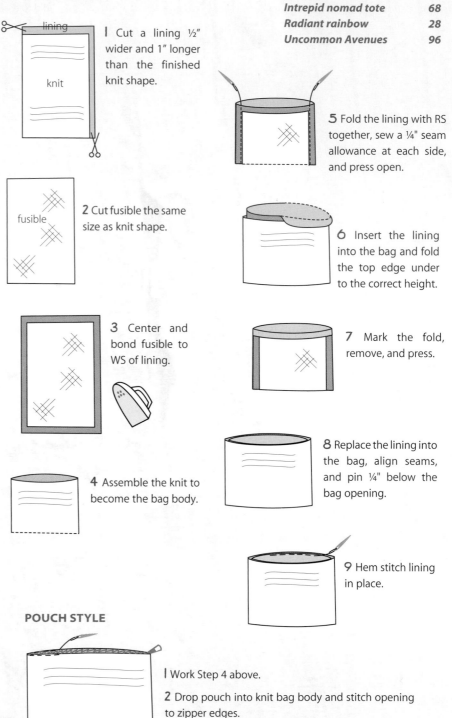

1 Cut a lining ½" wider and 1" longer than the finished knit shape.

2 Cut fusible the same size as knit shape.

3 Center and bond fusible to WS of lining.

4 Assemble the knit to become the bag body.

5 Fold the lining with RS together, sew a ¼" seam allowance at each side, and press open.

6 Insert the lining into the bag and fold the top edge under to the correct height.

7 Mark the fold, remove, and press.

8 Replace the lining into the bag, align seams, and pin ¼" below the bag opening.

9 Hem stitch lining in place.

POUCH STYLE

1 Work Step 4 above.

2 Drop pouch into knit bag body and stitch opening to zipper edges.

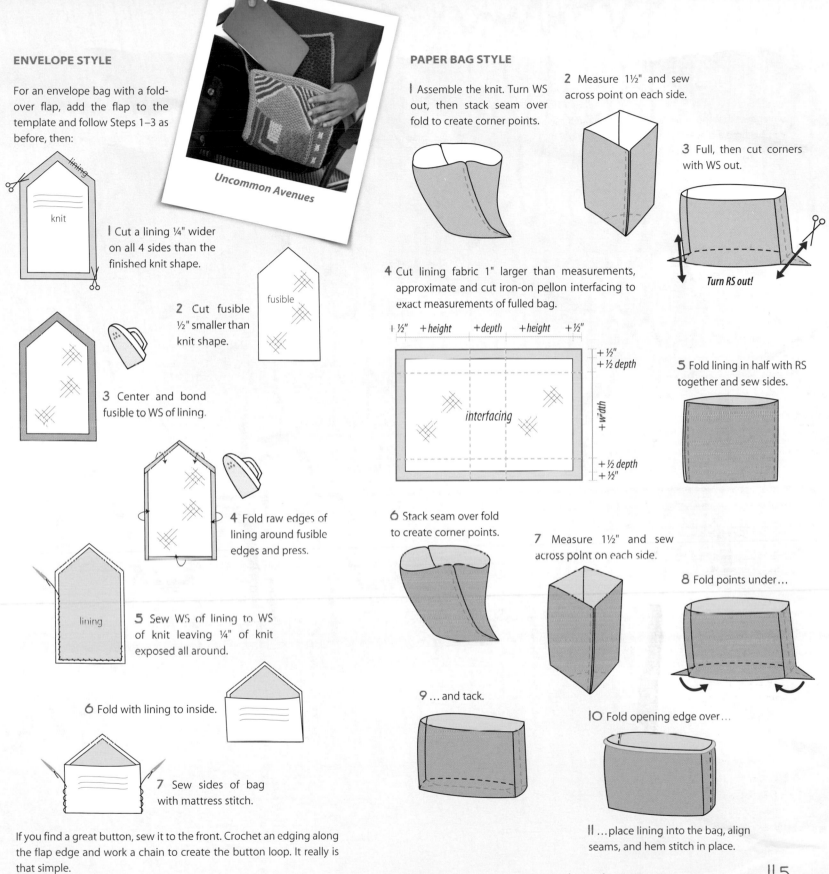

ENVELOPE STYLE

For an envelope bag with a fold-over flap, add the flap to the template and follow Steps 1–3 as before, then:

Uncommon Avenues

1 Cut a lining ¼" wider on all 4 sides than the finished knit shape.

2 Cut fusible ½" smaller than knit shape.

3 Center and bond fusible to WS of lining.

4 Fold raw edges of lining around fusible edges and press.

5 Sew WS of lining to WS of knit leaving ¼" of knit exposed all around.

6 Fold with lining to inside.

7 Sew sides of bag with mattress stitch.

If you find a great button, sew it to the front. Crochet an edging along the flap edge and work a chain to create the button loop. It really is that simple.

PAPER BAG STYLE

1 Assemble the knit. Turn WS out, then stack seam over fold to create corner points.

2 Measure 1½" and sew across point on each side.

3 Full, then cut corners with WS out.

Turn RS out!

4 Cut lining fabric 1" larger than measurements, approximate and cut iron-on pellon interfacing to exact measurements of fulled bag.

| ½" | + height | + depth | + height | + ½" |

interfacing

+ ½"
+ ½ depth

+ width

+ ½ depth
+ ½"

5 Fold lining in half with RS together and sew sides.

6 Stack seam over fold to create corner points.

7 Measure 1½" and sew across point on each side.

8 Fold points under…

9 … and tack.

10 Fold opening edge over…

11 …place lining into the bag, align seams, and hem stitch in place.

Basic Long Sleeve
Sizes based on Master Templates

I make sleeve decisions once the body is knit. Then I decide which design elements or different stitch patterns to include. Once the shoulder seams are sewn and steamed, I calculate the stitches for the sleeve cap and cuff and the rows for length. I knit top down, holding up the sleeve as I knit to check the length, but you are free to reverse the direction, start at the cuff, and increase to the shoulder.

Stitches/Rows	32"	36"	40"	44"	48"	52"

Stitches to cast on

Stitches/Rows	32"	36"	40"	44"	48"	52"
4/6	64	64	72	76	80	80
4.5/7	72	72	82	86	90	90
5/8	80	80	90	96	100	100
5.5/8	88	88	100	104	110	110
6/9	96	96	108	114	120	120

Work even for

32"	36"	40"	44"	48"	52"
¾"	1¾"	2¾"	3¼"	4"	5"

end with a WS row. Place markers at each end of last row. **Next row** Dec 1 at beginning and end of row. Work 1 row even.

Then Dec 1 each side

Stitches/Rows	32"	36"	40"	44"	48"	52"
4/6	E8R 2x E6R 14x	E6R 15x E4R 1x	E6R 10x E4R 8x	E6R 7x E4R 13x	E6R 1x E4R 21x	E4R 20x E2R 2x
4.5/7	E8R 4x E6R 14x	E8R 1x E6R 17x	E6R 11x E4R 10x	E6R 9x E4R 14x	E6R 2x E4R 23x	E4R 24x E2R 1x
5/8	E8R 6x E6R 14x	E8R 3x E6R 17x	E6R 15x E4R 8x	E6R 11x E4R 15x	E6R 8x E4R 18x	E6R 4x E4R 22x
5.5/8	E6R 22x	E6R 19x E4R 3x	E6R 9x E4R 17x	E6R 7x E4R 21x	E6R 2x E4R 27x	E4R 27x E2R 2x
6/9	E8R 3x E6R 21x	E6R 23x E4R 1x	E6R 12x E4R 16x	E6R 7x E4R 24x	E6R 3x E4R 29x	E4R 31x E2R 1x

Stitches remaining

Stitches/Rows	32"	36"	40"	44"	48"	52"
4/6	30	30	34	34	34	34
4.5/7	34	34	38	38	38	38
5/8	38	38	42	42	46	46
5.5/8	42	42	46	46	50	50
6/9	46	46	50	50	54	54

Work even if necessary until piece measures 2" less than desired length, or approximately

17½"	17½"	18"	19"	19"	19"

Return to sweater instructions for cuff finish OR finish as you wish.

knit in new directions → → →

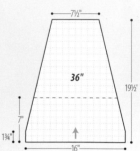

Key
E8R 2x = Every 8 rows, 2 times

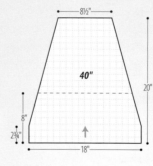

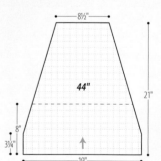

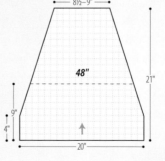

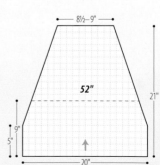

Make a stockinette swatch, or just begin with one sleeve based on the sweater's gauge. Make sure to measure row gauge after working the straight portion of the sleeve. Make any needed adjustments by changing needle size or rate of decrease.

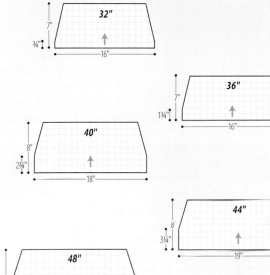

Basic Short Sleeve

Sizes based on Master Templates

Stitches/Rows	32"	36"	40"	44"	48"	52"

Stitches to cast on

Stitches/Rows	32"	36"	40"	44"	48"	52"
4/6	64	64	72	76	80	80
4.5/7	72	72	82	86	90	90
5/8	80	80	90	96	100	100
5.5/8	88	88	100	104	110	110
6/9	96	96	108	114	120	120

Work even for

32"	36"	40"	44"	48"	52"
¾"	1¾"	2¾"	3¼"	4"	5"

end with a WS row. Place markers **at** each end of last row. **Next row** Dec 1 at beginning and end of row. Work 1 row even.

Then Dec 1 each side

Stitches/Rows	32"	36"	40"	44"	48"	52"
4/6	E8R 1x E6R 5x	E6R 5x E2R 1x	E6R 5x E2R 1x	E6R 2x E4R 4x	E6R 3x E4R 3x	E4R 6x
4.5/7	E8R 4x E6R 2x	E6R 6x	E6R 4x E4R 3x	E6R 3x E4R 4x	E6R 3x E4R 4x	E4R 7x
5/8	E8R 6x	E8R 3x E6R 3x	E6R 3x E4R 6x	E6R 3x E4R 5x	E6R 4x E4R 4x	E4R 8x
5.5/8	E8R 6x	E8R 3x E6R 3x	E6R 1x E4R 9x	E4R 9x E2R 1x	E6R 2x E4R 7x	E4R 7x E2R 2x
6/9	E8R 4x E6R 4x	E6R 8x	E6R 4x E4R 6x	E4R 10x E2R 1x	E6R 2x E4R 8x	E4R 8x E2R 2x

Stitches remaining

Stitches/Rows	32"	36"	40"	44"	48"	52"
4/6	50	50	58	62	66	66
4.5/7	58	58	66	70	74	74
5/8	66	66	70	78	82	82
5.5/8	74	74	78	82	90	90
6/9	78	78	86	90	98	98

Work even if necessary until piece measures desired length, or approximately

7"	7"	8"	8"	9"	9"

Return to sweater instructions for cuff finish OR finish as you wish.

a journey into creativity →→→

Existing rows or stitches to I"	4	4.5	5	5.5	6
4	**1.0**				
4.5	.89	**1.0**			
5	.8	.9	**1.0**		
5.5	**.73**	.82	.91	**1.0**	
6	**.66**	**.75**	.83	.92	**1.0**
6.5	.62	.69	**.77**	.85	.92
7	.57	**.64**	.71	.79	.86
7.5	.53	.6	**.67**	**.73**	.8
8	**.5**	.56	.63	.69	**.75**
8.5		.53	.59	**.65**	.71
9		**.5**	.56	.61	**.67**
9.5			.53	.58	.63
10			**.5**	.55	.6
10.5				.52	.57
11				**.5**	.55
11.5					.52
12					**.5**

Ratio	Suggested rate of pick up
.5	1E2
.66	2E3
.75	3E4
1.0	1E1

1E2 Pick up 1 stitch for every 2 stitches or rows

Pick-up rates aren't always perfect, but knit fabric is forgiving, so approximate numbers work well. The upper table gives you standard stitch/row ratios. The lower table gives you pick-up rates for those color-coded ratios. Where there is no colored background for the stitch/row ratio, you can approximate the perfect rate by alternating between the rates above and below. For example, for a stitch/row ratio of .6, alternately pick up 2E3 and 1E2.

Pick-up rates & ratios

How . . . what . . . where . . . when

In creative knitting, you will pick up from edges — bound off, cast-on, selvedge, and selvedge with increases and decreases. There are guidelines for picking up stitches, which work — as long as you understand that you are working off the gauge of the existing fabric and creating a new fabric that may or may not have the same gauge.

Gauge is what matters here!
You will be using 2 gauges — the **existing gauge** of the edge (stitches or rows) and the **pick-up gauge** of the new fabric (stitches).

We make it a ratio
$$\frac{\text{pick-up gauge}}{\text{existing gauge}} \div$$

If you are knitting from a cast-on or bound-off edge and the 2 gauges are the same, you pick up a stitch in each existing stitch.

When we divide the **pick-up gauge** by the **existing gauge**, we get a percentage, shown as a **ratio** in the upper table. The lower table pairs ratios with the most common **pick-up rates**. Choose the one closest to your resulting percentage, pick up at that rate, and, if necessary either decrease or increase to your desired number of stitches in the following row. If your percentage falls between 2 on the chart, try alternating the rates below and above your ratio.

If there is a pattern change across the rows or stitches that changes the existing gauge, you may need to change rates.

pick up & knit in stitches... and in rows

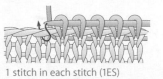

1 stitch in each stitch (1ES)

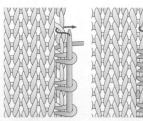

1 stitch in every other row (1E2R)   3 stitches in every 4 rows (3E4R)

When picking up or seaming a large number of stitches, it might help to divide the edge of the existing fabric into fourths and pick up or seam a quarter of the stitches within each section. Or you can break things down into smaller sections, which might be helpful — especially if the edge has assorted gauges.

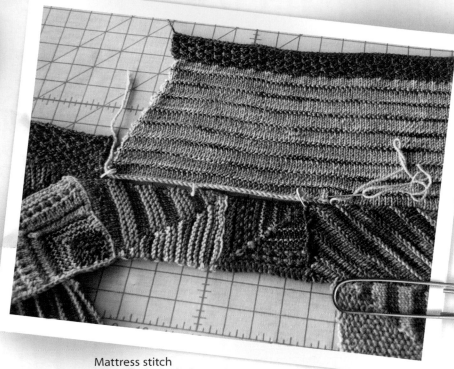

Mattress stitch
sleeve into armhole.

Sew shoulders and seam sleeves

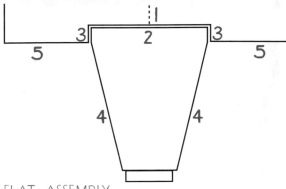

FLAT ASSEMBLY

1 Seam shoulder.
2 Center sleeve. Seam top of sleeve to armhole.
3 Seam underarm to sleeve.
4 Seam sleeve and...
5 ...seam front and back sides together.

When there is an underarm seam, I use a **flat assembly**: First I sew the shoulder seams, then lay the joined front and back pieces out flat with RS up. The sleeve is placed into the armhole, with the center point of the sleeve aligning with the shoulder seam. I seam the sleeves to the body along the entire armhole with mattress stitch. Next, I fold the garment at the shoulder seams, match and pin the sides from cuff to underarm to hem and sew those seams. I prefer to start at the underarm and work toward each cuff or hem so adjustments can be made if necessary.

At this point, steam to set the seams and joins and to make sure all the edges are even.

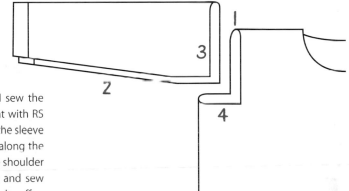

SET-IN ASSEMBLY

1 Seam shoulder.
2 Seam sleeve from first decrease to cuff.
3 Seam top of sleeve to body edge.
4 Seam underarm to sleeve.

When there is no underarm seam, I use a **set-in assembly**, seaming the sleeve before setting it into the armhole.

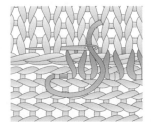

cast-on to rows   row to row

Techniques

Here

Elsewhere

Stitches

twisted cord

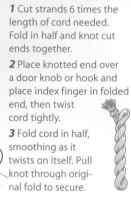

1 Cut strands 6 times the length of cord needed. Fold in half and knot cut ends together.

2 Place knotted end over a door knob or hook and place index finger in folded end, then twist cord tightly.

3 Fold cord in half, smoothing as it twists on itself. Pull knot through original fold to secure.

weaving in ends

To weave the carry above a stitch: Insert needle into stitch and under the end, then knit the stitch as usual.

To weave the carry below a stitch: Insert needle into stitch and the end, then knit the stitch as usual.
You can also *purl* above and below the end.

knit through the back loop (ktbl)

1 With right needle behind left needle and right leg of stitch, insert needle into stitch…

2 …and knit.

pick up & knit in stitches   and in rows

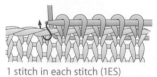
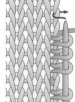

1 stitch in each stitch (1ES)

The ratio of picked-up stitches to rows is based on the pattern's stitch-to-row ratio. To test the formula, pick up stitches on your gauge swatch, work the border, and bind off.

1 stitch in every other row (1E2R)

3 stitches in every 4 rows (3E4R)

yarn over (yo)

Bring yarn under the needle to the front, over the needle to the back, and knit the next stitch.

After a knit, before a purl
Bring yarn under the needle to the front, over the needle to the back, then under the needle to the front, and purl the next stitch.

After a purl, before a knit
With yarn in front of the needle, bring it over the needle to the back, and knit the next stitch.

pick up & knit (PUK)

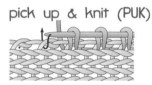

With RS facing and yarn in back, insert needle from front to back in center of edge stitch, catch yarn, and knit a stitch.
(See stockinette above, garter below.)

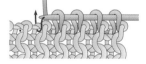

pick up & purl

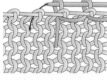

With WS facing and yarn in front, insert needle from back to front in center of edge stitch, catch yarn, and purl a stitch.

stitch orientation

This way | **Not this way**

It's essential to understand that every stitch should sit on the needle the correct way. The yarn coming from the previous stitch (the loop's right leg) is at the front of the needle. The yarn going to the following stitch (the loop's left leg) is at the back of the needle.

If a stitch does sit on the needle the wrong way, work into it as follows:

To knit the stitch
Insert right needle into stitch from front to back and knit the stitch.

To purl the stitch
Insert needle into stitch from back to front and purl the stitch.

butterfly

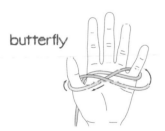

Wrap yarn in a figure-8 around fingers 6–8 times. To start knitting, pull tail, and yarn will release from center of ball.

Make small butterflies when using short lengths (less than 5 yards) of yarn for colorwork.

INCREASES

knit into front & back (kf&b)

1 Knit into front of next stitch on left needle, but do not pull the stitch off needle.

2 Take right needle to back, then knit through the back of the same stitch.

3 Pull stitch off left needle. Completed increase: 2 stitches from 1. This increase results in a purl bump after the knit stitch.

kf&b&f

Work **Steps 1 and 2**, then knit into front of stitch again—3 stitches from 1.

Make 1 (M1)

For a *left-slanting* increase (M1L), insert left needle from front to back under strand between last stitch knitted and first stitch on left needle. Knit, twisting strand by working into loop at back of needle.

The result is a left-slanting increase.

Or, for a *right-slanting* increase (M1R), insert left needle from back to front under strand between last stitch knitted and first stitch on left needle. Knit, twisting strand by working into loop at front of needle.

The result is a right-slanting increase.

purl into front & back (pf&b)

1 Purl into front of next stitch, but do not pull stitch off needle.

2 Take right needle to back, then through back of same stitch, from left to right…

3 …and purl.

4 Pull stitch off left needle. Completed increase: 2 stitches from 1 stitch. This increase results in a purl bump before the stitch on the RS.

pf&b&f

Work **Steps 1 and 2**, then purl into front of stitch again—3 stitches from 1.

DECREASES

SSK

1 Slip 2 stitches separately to right needle as if to knit.

2 Slip left needle into these 2 stitches from left to right and knit them together:

2 stitches become 1.
The result is a left-slanting decrease.

SSSK

Work same as SSK EXCEPT: **1** Slip 3 stitches…. **2** Slip left needle into these 3 stitches… 3 stitches become 1. The result is a left-slanting double decrease.

k2tog (k3tog)

1 Insert right needle into first 2 (3) stitches on left needle, beginning with second (third) stitch from end of left needle.

2 Knit these 2 (3) stitches together as if they were 1. The result is a right-slanting double decrease.

DECREASES

p2tog

1 Insert right needle into first 2 stitches on left needle.

2 Purl these 2 stitches together as if they were 1. The result is a right-slanting decrease.

S2KP2, S2-KI-P2SSO

1 Slip 2 stitches together to right needle as if to knit.

2 Knit next stitch.

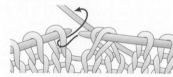

3 Pass 2 slipped stitches over knit stitch and off right needle: 3 stitches become 1; the center stitch is on top.
The result is a centered double decrease.

SK2P, S1-k2tog-psso

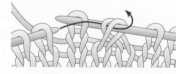

1 Slip 1 stitch knitwise. **2** Knit next 2 stitches together. **3** Pass the slipped stitch over the k2tog: 3 stitches become 1; the right stitch is on top. The result is a left-slanting double decrease.

CROCHET

single crochet (SC)

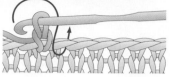

1 Insert hook into a stitch, catch yarn, and pull up a loop. Catch yarn and pull through the loop on the hook.
2 Insert hook into next stitch to the left.

3 Catch yarn and pull through the stitch; 2 loops on hook.

4 Catch yarn and pull through both loops on hook; 1 single crochet completed. Repeat Steps 2–4.

double crochet (DC)

1 Insert hook into a stitch, catch yarn, and pull up a loop. Chain 3 (counts as first double crochet).
2 Yarn over, insert hook into next stitch to the left (as shown). Catch yarn and pull through stitch only; 3 loops on hook.

3 Catch yarn and pull through 2 loops on hook.

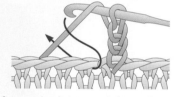

4 Catch yarn and pull through remaining 2 loops on hook. Repeat Steps 2–4.

backward single crochet

1 Insert hook into a stitch, catch yarn, and pull up a loop. Catch yarn and pull a loop through the loop on the hook.
2 Insert hook into next stitch to right.

3 Catch yarn and pull through stitch only (as shown). As soon as hook clears the stitch, flip your wrist (and hook). There are 2 loops on the hook, and the just-made loop is to the front of hook (left of old loop).

4 Catch yarn and pull through both loops on hook; 1 backward single crochet completed.

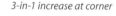

5 Continue working to the right, repeating Steps 2–4.

slip-stitch crochet

1 Insert the hook into a stitch, catch yarn, and pull up a loop.

2 Insert hook into the next stitch to the left, catch yarn, and pull through both the stitch and the loop on the hook; 1 slip stitch completed. Repeat Step 2.

chain stitch

1 Make a slip knot to begin. **2** Catch yarn and draw through loop on hook (left). First chain made (right). Repeat Step 2.

half double crochet (hdc)

1 Insert hook into a stitch, catch yarn, and pull up a loop. Chain 2 (counts as first half double crochet).

2 Yarn over, insert hook into next stitch to the left (as shown). Catch yarn and pull through stitch only; 3 loops on hook.

3 Catch yarn and pull through all 3 loops on hook: 1 half double crochet complete. Repeat Steps 2–3.

crochet corners

3-in-1 increase at corner

3-in-1 increase: Work 3 crochet stitches into 1 stitch. This rate of increase, repeated each row, works with all of the common crochet stitches.

2-to-1 decrease: Work a stitch to its last step, work the next stitch to its last step, then pull yarn through all loops on hook (shown above in single crochet).

SLIPS

slip purlwise (sl p-wise)

1 Insert right needle into next stitch on left needle from back to front (as if to purl).

2 Slide stitch from left needle to right needle. Stitch orientation does not change (right leg of stitch loop is at front of needle).

The stitch slipped purlwise can be a knit or a purl.

slip knitwise (sl k-wise)

1 Insert right needle into next stitch on left needle from front to back (as if to knit).

2 Slide stitch from left needle to right needle. Stitch orientation changes (right leg of stitch loop is at back of needle).

The stitch slipped knitwise can be a knit or a purl.

BIND OFF

3-needle bind-off

Bind-off ridge on wrong side

1 With stitches on 2 needles, place *RS together.* *Knit 2 stitches together (1 from front needle and 1 from back needle, as shown); repeat from * once more.

2 With left needle, pass first stitch on right needle over second stitch and off right needle.

3 Knit next 2 stitches together.

4 Repeat Steps 2 and 3, end by drawing yarn through last stitch. (See Fasten off).

fasten off

Work bind-off until only 1 stitch remains on right needle. If this is the last stitch of a row, cut yarn and fasten off stitch as shown above. Otherwise, this is the first stitch of the next section of knitting.

K the K's . . .

Here's what you do when we say: "Knit the knit stitches and purl the purl stitches."

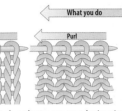 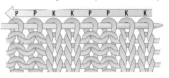

In stockinette stitch, when you see knit stitches, you knit. When you see purl stitches, you purl.

In rib, what you do is **the same** as what you see below the needle.

K the P's . . .

Here's what you do when we say: "Knit the purl stitches and purl the knit stitches."

In seed stitch, what you do is **the opposite** of what you see below the needle.

USEFUL ABBREVIATIONS

CC contrasting color
cn cable needle
cm centimeter(s)
dec decrease
dpn double pointed needle(s)
g gram(s)
" inch(es)
inc increase
k knit
LH left-hand
M1 Make one stitch (increase)
m meter(s)

mm millimeter(s)
MC main color
oz ounce(s)
p purl
pm place marker
psso pass slipped stitch(es) over
RH right-hand
RS right side(s)
sc single crochet
sl slip
SKP slip, knit, psso
SK2P slip, k2tog, psso

ssk slip, slip, knit these 2 sts tog
ssp slip, slip, purl these 2 sts tog
st(s) stitch(es)
tbl through back of loop(s)
tog together
WS wrong side(s)
wyib with yarn in back
wyif with yarn in front
x times
yd(s) yard(s)
yo yarn over

Yarns

Long-repeat yarns shown in color

2

Fine

CLAUDIA HAND PAINTED YARNS *Fingering* 100% extra fine merino wool; 50g (1.75oz); 160m (175yds)

KOIGU WOOL DESIGNS *KPPPM* 100% merino wool; 50g (1.75oz); 155m (170yds)

3

Light

BERROCO *Ultra Alpaca Light* 50% super fine alpaca, 50% Peruvian wool; 50g (1.75oz); 133m (144yds)

CASCADE YARNS *220 Sport* 100% Peruvian Highland wool; 50g (1.75oz); 150m (164yds)

FREIA HANDPAINT YARNS *Ombre Sport* 100% wool; 75g (2.65oz); 198m (217yds)

FREIA HANDPAINT YARNS *Semi-Solid Sport* 100% wool; 50g (1.75oz); 78m (85yds)

KRAEMER YARNS *Tatamy Tweed DK* 45% cotton, 55% acrylic; 100g (3.5oz); 229m (250yds)

MALABRIGO *Arroyo* 100% superwash merino wool; 100g (3.5oz); 306m (335yds)

MALABRIGO *Silky Merino* 50% silk, 50% baby merino wool; 50g (1.75oz); 137m (150yds)

NORO *Silk Garden Lite* 45% silk, 45% kid mohair, 10% lambswool; 50g (1.75oz); 128m (137yds)

ROWAN *Baby Merino Silk DK* 66% merino superwash wool, 34% tussah silk; 50g (1.75oz); 135m (147yds)

4

Medium

ARAUCANIA *Nature Wool* 100% wool; 100g (3.5oz); 221m (242yds)

BROWN SHEEP *Lamb's Pride Worsted* 85% wool, 15% mohair; 100g (3.5oz); 174m (190yds)

CASCADE YARNS *220* 100% Peruvian Highland wool; 100g (3.5oz); 200m (220yds)

CASCADE YARNS *Casablancao* 57% wool, 24% silk, 19% mohair; 100g (3.5oz); 200m (220yds)

CASCADE YARNS *Souk* 55% silk, 45% wool; 100g (3.5oz); 200m (220yds)

CLAUDIA HAND PAINTED YARNS *Worsted* 100% wool; 100g (3.5oz); 134m (146yds)

FIESTA YARNS *Boomerang* 100% extrafine superwash merino; 113g (4oz); 229m (250yds)

FIESTA YARNS *Gelato* 100% rayon; 85g (3oz); 240m (262yds)

JOJOLAND *Rhythm* 100% wool; 50g (1.75oz); 100m (110yds)

MALABRIGO *Merino Worsted* 100% merino wool; 100g (3.5oz); 192m (210yds)

NORO *Kureyon* 100% superwash wool; 50g (1.75oz); 100m (109yds)

PRISM YARNS *Symphony* 80% merino, 10% cashmere; 56g (2oz); 108m (118yds)

RED HEART BOUTIQUE *Treasure* 70% acrylic, 30% wool; 100g (3.5oz); 138m (151yds)

SKACEL COLLECTION *Simpliworsted by HiKoo* 55% merino superwash, 28% acrylic, 17% nylon; 100g (3.5oz); 128m (140yds)

UNIVERSAL YARN *Wisdom Poems Silk* 75% wool, 25% silk; 50g (1.75oz); 100m (110yds)

UNIVERSAL YARN *Classic Shades* 70% acrylic, 30% wool; 100g (3.5oz); 180m (197yds)

Yarn Weight Categories

Yarn Weight

Super Fine	Fine	Light	Medium	Bulky	Super Bulky

Also called

Sock Fingering Baby	Sport Baby	DK Light-Worsted	Worsted Afghan Aran	Chunky Craft Rug	Bulky Roving

Stockinette Stitch Gauge Range 10cm/4 inches

27 sts to 32 sts	23 sts to 26 sts	21 sts to 24 sts	16 sts to 20 sts	12 sts to 15 sts	6 sts to 11 sts

Recommended needle (metric)

2.25 mm to 3.25 mm	3.25 mm to 3.75 mm	3.75 mm to 4.5 mm	4.5 mm to 5.5 mm	5.5 mm to 8 mm	8 mm and larger

Recommended needle (US)

1 to 3	3 to 5	5 to 7	7 to 9	9 to 11	11 and larger

Throughout this book, the photo caption describes the yarns and colors in the photograph. If a yarn is not available, its yardage and content information will help in making a substitution. Locate the Yarn Weight and Stockinette Stitch Gauge Range over 10cm to 4" on the chart. Compare that range with the information on the yarn label to find an appropriate yarn. These are guidelines only for commonly used gauges and needle sizes in specific yarn categories.

Conversion chart

centimeters		0.394		inches
grams		0.035		ounces
inches	**X**	2.54	**=**	centimeters
ounces		28.6		grams
meters		1.1		yards
yards		.91		meters

Equivalent weights

¾	oz		20 g
1	oz		28 g
1½	oz		40 g
1¾	oz		50 g
2	oz		57 g
3½	oz		100 g

Needles/Hooks

US	MM	HOOK
0	2	A
1	2.25	B
2	2.75	C
3	3.25	D
4	3.5	E
5	3.75	F
6	4	G
7	4.5	7
8	5	H
9	5.5	I
10	6	J
10½	6.5	K
11	8	L
13	9	M
15	10	N
17	12.75	

Approximate yardages
Our Long-Sleeve Template

SIZE	32	36	40	44	48	52
5 stitches/ 7 rows	**1200**	**1250**	**1375**	**1500**	**1625**	**1675**
5.5 stitches/ 8 rows	**1325**	**1375**	**1500**	**1650**	**1775**	**1850**
6 stitches/ 9 rows	**1450**	**1500**	**1650**	**1875**	**1950**	**2000**
Approximate square inches of fabric	1129	1173	1279	1410	1518	1564

This chart is an estimate for our template worked in stockinette fabric. *Row gauge differences* Let's consider that you are working a garter-based or slip-stitch fabric; you will knit more rows in each inch, therefore you will need more yarn. If your gauge swatch is 5 stitches by 10 rows, compare it to the 5/7 gauge. There are 35 (5×7) stitches in a square inch in the stockinette swatch, but yours has 50 (5×10). Divide your stitches per square inch by those in the stockinette swatch ($50 \div 35 = 1.43$). So, multiply the yarn required for your size at the gauge of 5/7 by 1.43 for the approximate yardage you will need—almost a third more yarn. Rows count!

Our Sleeveless Template *(APPROXIMATELY 66% OF ABOVE)*

SIZE	32	36	40	44	48	52
5 stitches/ 7 rows	**800**	**825**	**900**	**1000**	**1075**	**1100**
5.5 stitches/ 8 rows	**875**	**925**	**1000**	**1100**	**1175**	**1225**
6 stitches/ 9 rows	**950**	**1000**	**1100**	**1250**	**1300**	**1325**
Approximate square inches of fabric	671	715	759	844	920	966

a journey into creativity →→→

This template is an essential tool for making most of the garments in this book. It takes 3 simple steps to turn these mini-templates into the life-size template you will use:

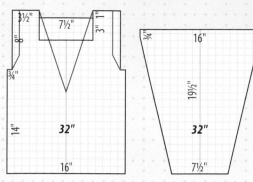

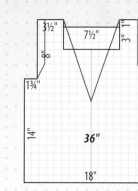

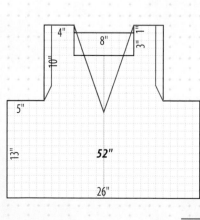

MASTER TEMPLATES

1 Choose your size

2 Enlarge to life-size on fabric: Pellon or muslin

3 Make any style changes to the life-size template

Style changes will be shown in a Master Template box, usually at the beginning of the instructions.

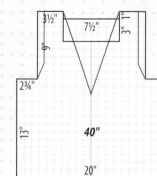

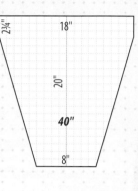

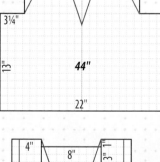

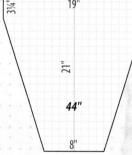

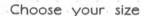

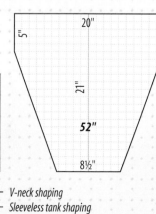

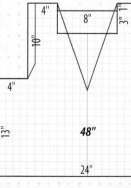

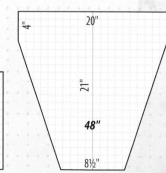

—— V-neck shaping
—— Sleeveless tank shaping

For life-size template: Go direct to Pellon (see page 15)
OR enlarge template 1286% or until ☐ = 1" and transfer to muslin.

Customizing the template with A-line shaping

Shape your knit in the underarm panels for added width at the waist and hips. Because the panels are knit sideways, shaping can easily be done with short rows. Most any stitch pattern can be used.

Spacing the short-row turns evenly along the length of the rows makes any distortion of a stitch pattern less noticeable as the width increases from armhole to hemline. In most cases, 2 to 4 short-row pairs are worked close to the armhole, spaced 5 stitches apart. For a wider wedge, additional pairs of short rows can be worked into the panel.

This sample starts with 40 stitches of seed stitch worked for 1", then 3 pairs of short rows are turned at stitches 30, 20, and 10. Notice how you really cannot tell where the W&Ts are.

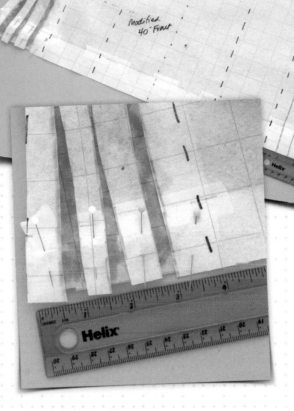

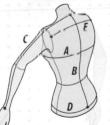

A Bust ——
B Body length ——
C Center back to cuff
(arm slightly bent) ——
D Hip ——
E Shoulder width ——

The template size — 32", 36", 40", etc. — is the circumference of the garment. When choosing the size to make, add from 1"–4" to your body measurement to allow for ease.

Working the template

Using your template, you can easily adjust the panels at the underarms with a slash-and-spread technique.

Look at the template and decide how much wider you want it to be at the hem. Remember, you'll be placing this shaping at both sides of back and front. As few as 2 short-row pairs in each of 4 places will add 16 rows to the hemline — this may be enough to do the job without drawing any attention to the shaping.

At the underarm on the template, slash from hem toward underarm in 2 to 3 places, then spread the hem to the desired width. You can then use this as your map (see photo).

For stockinette with vertical garter ridges, place 1 short-row pair in each stockinette area as needed. The garter ridges converge toward the armhole and flare at the hemline for an added design element.

This book has been an amazing journey and there are so many people I want to thank who continue to inspire this crazy creative life I'm so fortunate to live.

My thanks go out especially to Benjamin Levisay who always believes in me, Elaine Rowley, whose vision and passion have made this more than I could have ever imagined, Rick Mondragon's overall genius, Alexis Xenakis—Photographer Extraordinaire, and all of the XRX staff who worked so hard to make this dream come true.

To my Mom who started me in the right direction in so many ways, my Dad who taught me the meaning of "I can make that," my husband Page—my heart and soul, whom I'm so blessed to share this journey with, my BFF Elle who still makes me want to be a better woman, and a shout out to my home slice.

Also, many thanks to Team Stitches, my fiber family world-wide, and all of my students who inspire me daily. I love you all.